FROM
THE
COURTS

TO
THE
STREETZ

THE AUTOBIOGRAPHY OF:

ISAAC " IKE-MOE " WILLIAMS

Printed in the United States of America. First Printing, 2010

ISBN 978-0-692-90168-7

U Can Publishing

2230 Hatcher St.

Dallas, TX 75215

Table of Contents

Dedication...5

Introduction: Politics...7

Chapter 1: East Dallas..11

Chapter 2: My Father..17

Chapter 3: My Family..25

Chapter 4: Hoop Dreams....................................37

Chapter 5: Biddie Ball...47

Chapter 6: Back To The Old Neighborhood..................................51

Chapter 7: Opportunity Arrives.......................63

Chapter 8: The Shift (Becoming Intrigued By the Streets).....69

Chapter 9: Gaining Recognition.......................73

Chapter 10: Proposition 48...............................79

Chapter 11: The Scare...85

Chapter 12: Back On The Team.......................91

Chapter 13: The Pressure.................................101

Chapter 14: Politics As Usual........................105

Chapter 15: Change..109

Chapter 16: The Betrayal..................................113

Chapter 17: See It Through...125

Chapter 18: The Dope Game...133

Chapter 19: 2 Feet in The Game...139

Chapter 20: Game Over..149

Chapter 21: Knowledge of Self...159

Chapter 22: The Disappointment..169

Chapter 23: The Ten Year Plan...175

About the Author..185

Dedication

This book is dedicated to the people that have inspired and contributed to the beliefs and morals that I have lived with and struggled in. To The people that have been right there with me through the good, the bad, and ugly.

To the people that have set the example before and during my time. To the leaders that I have never met, but have listened to over the years. To all my family members, friends, Brughs, and the ones who have made the transition. Each of you have a played a major role in my life that has shaped me into the man I am today. And for that, I thank you.

Introduction: Politics

There is something that's really been heavy on my heart for many years, and I need to get it off my chest. I have been wanting to say this for a long time. And as a man, there are just some things I don't understand, and I probably never will understand.

I was taught as a kid that you had to be a man of principles, values, and morals. You had to stand for something. Nothing is given to you, and you have to work hard for what you want out of life. And, I was told, that this is what builds character in a man.

But in life and family, this is not so true. There is a word out there that's called "Favoritism" aka "Politics." This is when a man gets rewarded for who he knows, and not his talents. As a man, and as an athlete, I just can't respect that. Never did, and I never will. Unfortunately, I was a product of this kind of abuse coming up.

This poisoned my life as a man, and as a basketball player. I had to sit back and watch kids that weren't better than me, or some of the other kids, and they would get the starting position or make the team, because of who their parents were or the color of their skin. This poison is what made me fall out of love with the game. This was my first heartbreak, so to speak.

I was raised on a code that stated that the best man gets to play, and if you ain't good enough, you go get it right, and then come back. But, to make a long story short, pretty much everywhere I go nowadays , I get asked the question, Ike-Moe, you made it all the way to the Lakers, why did you did you stop? Why didn't you get the millions of dollars? What happened?

And every time someone asks me these questions, the shit would hurt. The pain was so bad, because it was something I just didn't know how to explain at the time. And to be honest, I didn't want to explain, because I didn't want to go back and visit that pain anymore. So I never opened up.

And by not opening up, this pain sent me into a downward spiral in life, which led me into the street life where I was lost and had no hope. We will get more into that in the book, but I thank God I was fortunate enough to rebound from that lifestyle. I'm blessed man, because I know some people who didn't.

From that, I truly understand what depression is, and what other athletes with the same story I have are going through. How do I know? Because I am around them on a consistent basis, and we share the same pain and the same story.

It's tough when people put you on a pedestal when they think you are going to make it big. And then when you don't, they turn their back on you and treat you like ain't shit. That's a hard reality to face when you are young and, to be honest, the shit is devastating. Excuse my French y'all, I got to get this out!!!

This is why I feel this book, <u>From The Court To The Streetz, The Story Of My Life</u>, is so relevant. This is why I'm putting it all out there, and showing the mistakes I made, where I went wrong, and when I should have listened to the people who cared and I didn't.

I'm exposing my life and putting it all out there, because I know there's another Ike-Moe somewhere out there in the world, lost and who doesn't know how to find hope, headed down the same road I took. And I don't want to see that happen. I want to make that bridge easier for that next man to cross. I don't want to see him or them make the same mistakes I made, because they might not be so lucky.

I hope y'all support this book because this is bigger than me. I'm telling it all, "No Hoes Bared". Those who know, know, and those who don't, I hope you find my story helpful and uplifting. And for those people who are worried and fit the description, we good. I will not put anything in this book that would incriminate anyone. This is a book of love!!!

All proceeds of this book will go to my foundation, Unlocked Mindz, to kick start the clinic that we will be having every summer. This program will be mentoring high school athletes, getting them ready for college, and helping them make the right choices during college recruiting. Most of all, having a Plan B in life.

Peace!!

Chapter 1: East Dallas

As the sun began to rise above the beautiful orange and blue sky, I fell into deep meditation. The smell of frankincense and myrrh clouded the room. As my thoughts grew deeper, I asked myself, "What can I do to give back to humanity, and be a service to mankind?"

It dawned on me as clear as day. I picked up the phone and dialed Andy. Andy is a short, heavy-set Jewish guy in his mid-50's that blogs for XM radio. He's originally from Boston, but he resides here in Dallas now.

"I think I'm ready," I answered when Andy answered the phone.

"I don't understand."

I could hear the confusion in his voice.

"I think I'm ready to tell my story and put the past behind."

The confusion was gone and there was an eagerness in his tone now.

"I'm happy for you. When do you want to get started?"

It was past time for waiting.

"I would like to get started today."

Andy and I agreed to meet at 10 am. A couple of hours later, the phone rang. It was Andy letting me know he was downstairs. I went down to let him up the elevator.

"Ike, you look like you should have been a football player," Andy laughed.

He wasn't the first person to tell me that.

"Really? It's funny that you say that. Dennis Franchione, our head football coach at New Mexico, used to always tease me and say, 'Ike, I want you to come out and be my tight end. 'The crazy thing about it is that he was serious as hell."

Andy laughed even harder, and it was infectious. The two of us were laughing together as we got off the elevator. We got into the house and Andy sat his briefcase on the floor before laying his notepad and tape recorder on the table.

"What was it like growing up in East Dallas?"

My mind went back to those days.

"It was rough. But If you've seen one ghetto, you've seen them all. In the ghetto, there's a code you must live by. If you violate that code, you suffer the consequences. When I was a kid, I knew a guy that got killed over one dollar. Some people would ask, 'Why would someone get killed over a dollar? That's nonsense.' That might be true, but the guy that killed him begged to differ. He told the authorities, it wasn't about the dollar. It was about the principles of the situation."

All that Andy could manage to say in reply to that was, "Wow."

I shook my head.

"Yes. East Dallas was, and still is, a poverty-stricken neighborhood. It was a tough place to live, more mentally than physically. Statistics show that the life expectancy of a black male living in the ghetto is sixteen."

Andy positioned himself on the stool.

"Unbelievable."

I shrugged.

"It is. Growing up in East Dallas was tough, but at that time, I knew no different."

Andy seemed genuinely curious.

"Why?"

It was a good question.

"The ghetto was all that I knew at the time. I had no clue what life was like on the other side of town until desegregation and we were bussed into middle-class communities to attend school."

I could see that this was a topic that interested Andy.

"What was it like attending school outside of your neighborhood?"

There weren't enough words to describe it, honestly, but I tried.

"It was a different experience. To be honest, it was a culture shock. It was a gift and a curse. The gift was being exposed to a different culture. The curse was trying to adapting to a new culture. Many days, I went home frustrated. Do you know what it's like when you have to wear the same shirt on Tuesday that your brother wore on Monday? Do you know what it's like to have to share the same underwear and socks with your siblings? Do you know what it's like to go to school and be embarrassed to take your shoes off during recess because your big toe is sticking out of your socks and your shoes have an odor that would run a skunk off? This type of abuse will mess a child's psyche up, man."

The room went silent.

"Was growing up in East Dallas that bad?"

I smiled.

"No, it wasn't. Actually, I had some fun times growing up there."

He seemed relieved.

"Where is East Dallas located?"

The streets I listed off to him were just names to him, but to me they brought back images of territory I'd travelled so often I knew them by heart.

"East Dallas is pretty much divided into four sections: Fitzhugh to Spring, Spring to Hatcher, Projects to the Hill, and the Hill to East Grand. In fear of the consequences of war, all the sections pretty much got along and respected one another, but it wasn't wise to get caught in another territory if you weren't invited. I remember one instance when a couple of guys out of our section were caught out-of-pocket in Marshall square. You would have thought they were running for the U.S. Olympics. They got to Church's Chicken in 0.3 seconds."

Andy's laughter filled the room.

"That's hilarious."

His tone became serious again as he asked the next question.

"How do you survive in a place like East Dallas?"

It was a simple code.

"You have to respect and treat others the way you wanna be treated."

Andy nodded.

"Enough said."

Chapter 2: My Father

"Moving forward. Are your parents still living?"

An image flashed into my mind of my mother and my father.

"My father died when I was 14. My mother is still living."

Andy's next question didn't surprise me.

"How did your father die?"

My answer did surprise him, though.

"He died in a car wreck. A guy fell asleep behind the wheel and ran into him head-on."

Andy shook his head.

"Wow!"

I continued the story.

"It was devastating. What was more devastating, though, was the pain that was on the guy's face who killed my father as he asked for forgiveness. As I watched the tears run down his face, I felt a feeling I've never felt before. My heart was crushed, but the anger that I once had for him faded away. I looked at him as he lay there in his hospital bed and thought to myself, 'this is a good man that made a mistake. He's no killer. He deserves a second chance. It was an accident.' "

I could see tears form in Andy's eyes as he looked at me and smiled.

"You forgave him."

I nodded my head.

"Yes. We forgave him and dropped all charges."

Andy wiped the tears from his face.

"Wow. That says a lot."

His tone softened for a moment.

"I'm sorry to hear about what happened to your father."

My own voice softened as I told Andy the truth.

"It's okay. When I heard he passed, I only cried twice. Once when I heard the news, and once at the funeral."

Confusion was written all over Andy's face.

"Why?"

I looked Andy in the eye.

"I didn't like my daddy for the things he did to us."

Andy was quiet, and I knew he was waiting for me to explain.

"The first time I ever laid eyes on my father, I think I was about 4 or 5 years old. I can remember this slim, clean cut man standing in front of our house. He was about 6'3", dressed all in white, wearing black steel toe boots. He was fresh out of prison."

I stopped for a moment and closed my eyes.

"I can remember asking my mother, 'Who's that man?' She said, 'Son, that's your father.'"

Andy's eyebrows were raised.

"What did he go to prison for?"

I looked at Andy and paused for a second.

"He beat a murder case in self-defense and took a plea on a lesser charge."

The room went silent again. I decided to keep going with the story.

"From that day forward, life was never the same."

I think it was hard for someone like Andy to imagine the kind of life I'd lived.

"I don't understand."

I looked at Andy and smiled.

"This was the beginning of my dislike for my father."

Andy's face grew serious.

"What type of man was your father?"

I answered calmly, but even after all these years I could still feel the helpless rage as I watched my father abuse my mother.

"My father was an alcoholic. And he was abusive. The things I watched him do to my mother made me want to kill him. Not only me, but my brothers, too."

I could tell Andy was caught off guard again.

"You have brothers?"

"Yes, I do. I have four brothers, but I have a different father from them."

Andy nodded.

"Okay, I got it. He was your biological father. Now I understand why your pain is so deep."

I wanted to speak, but the words wouldn't come out. Andy walked around the table to pat me on my shoulder.

"It's okay."

I looked at Andy.

"He only told me he loved me once, and that was two weeks before he died."

There were tears in his eyes as Andy looked at me.

"Wow."

I looked away again. It was too hard to say this and look at him.

"Up until I was 12 years of age, I wet the bed. The school counselors believed the cause was my nerves."

Andy leaned back on the stool and shook his head in disbelief.

"Are you serious?"

I sighed heavily.

"Yes, I am. I was terrified of my father. I remember one day, my father suspected my mother of cheating. He pulled me out of the screen door by my arm. He pulled this gun out from under his shirt and shot a black cat in the head. Then he turned and looked at me, frowned, and said, 'This is what I'll do to a nigga'. I was traumatized, watching that cat's body turn as the bullet pierced his head."

Andy's voice echoed loudly from the walls.

"Are you kidding me?"

I wish I had been.

"No, I'm not."

Andy shook his head again and silently sat back down on the stool. You could have heard a pin drop on the floor, everything was so quiet. My thoughts drifted back into the past and the present faded away.

It was a hot summer Texas night. No air was moving. I heard my mother's cry over the roar of my father's vicious bite. He was tearing into her like a beast tears into their prey.

His voice was angry and the look he gave us was filled with vengeance.

"Come on out, now. I want to see how tough ya'll are."

He stood behind the kitchen door with his .38 special cocked and loaded. I can still remember the look on my oldest brother, Greg's, face as he stared silently toward the door. He was frozen, cold as ice!!

I heard Andy's voice calling me back into the present and the past began to fade away.

"Ike, are you okay? Are you okay?"

I looked at Andy and smiled, but I could still feel the fear coiling in my belly the same as it had that summer night so long ago.

"I'm okay. One thing good I can say about my father. He was a great provider. Our lights never went off, and we never missed a meal."

Andy looked at me. His face was carefully neutral. He voice was relaxed.

"Tell me more about your mother."

Chapter 3: My Family

"My momma. I put her through so much pain, man. Sometimes we don't know what we put our parents through until we become parents. There is nothing bad I can say about my momma."

My voice started to crack as I remembered everything she'd gone through to raise us.

"I remember when my momma used to wear the same clothes to work every day so we could have clothes to wear to school."

I fight back the tears that come as I talk about the sacrifices she made.

"I remember watching her get up at 4 o'clock in the morning to catch the bus to work so we could have food on the table. Times were real back then."

I look at Andy.

"I can remember when we wore the same drawers, same clothes, and same holey-ass socks, but one thing is fo-sho, and two things are for certain. Nobody in the family went hungry. She would take food out of her own freezer to feed her family."

Andy shook his head.

"Wow."

He paused for just a moment out of respect before he went on to the next question.

"Tell me more about your sisters."

There wasn't a lot I could tell him about them.

"I really didn't know my sisters that well. Kay, my oldest sister, she came around some. She was older than me, but she passed away. My other sister, we only met once, when my Daddy passed on. I was about 14. We talked for a little while, but it didn't last long. I seriously thought we were going to get to know each other, but unfortunately it didn't work out that way."

I smiled but I could still remember how badly this hurt.

"The crazy thing about it is that I always thought about her as a child. I used to always wonder what she looked like, and it really hurt me that we couldn't get to know each other."

Andy looked at me to make sure I was okay and shook his head before going on.

"Tell me more about your brothers."

A warm smile crossed my face.

"Where do I start? I'm very fortunate to have good brothers. The things I learned from them and the sacrifices they made for me, words can't explain. They gave me a lot of knowledge but, unfortunately, I had to go to the streets to get the rest."

Andy clearly is puzzled by this statement.

"Why?"

How could I explain the emptiness that haunted my youth?

"Because there was still a void. There was still something missing.

Not to discredit my brothers, but it was something I had to do to become complete."

Andy was shaking his head in confusion.

"My father was a street guy and I didn't really know him. But, believe it or not, I learned a lot about him from being in the streets."

Andy looked so puzzled. I knew this was hard for someone who hadn't been there to get.

"I don't understand."

It was even harder for me to explain.

"See, a lot of the guys my father hung out with were still living. When we met in passing, they would tell me stories about him. Some good, some bad."

The confusion cleared from Andy's face.

"Now, I understand."

I nodded.

"Those stories gave me a better understanding of who I am today. Many people get the streets misconstrued. They don't understand that there are actually good people in the streets. By all means, please don't get me wrong, I'm in no way condoning being on the streets. I'm just speaking from my personal experiences."

Andy smiled.

"I understand."

He adjusted his glasses before continuing the interview.

"Are you the youngest of the five?"

I smiled and nodded.

"Yes. Being the youngest came with privileges."

It was clear Andy was lost again.

"I don't understand."

I thought about everything my brothers did for me and I knew there was no real way to make somebody who didn't have that get it.

"A lot of the pressure my brothers had to face, I didn't have to."

"Why?" Andy asked.

I felt nothing but gratitude for what they'd done for me.

"They made the ultimate sacrifice. Two of my brothers gave up their basketball dreams so I could pursue mine. They went to work so we could have food on the table."

Andy looked alert and leaned forward.

"Really? Tell me more."

I was proud to share this with him.

"My brother Byron was a sophomore, and my brother Baboo was a junior. They both played varsity basketball for James Madison High School in the mid-80's. They were both good. All of my brothers were good. I learned a lot about the game from watching them."

Andy whistled.

"Wow."

I smiled and kept going.

"I borrowed the hustle from my brother, Byron, and the aggressiveness from my brother, Baboo. The jump shot from my brother, Howard, and the work ethic and court awareness from my brother, Greg."

Andy made some notes.

"Oh, wow. Who's the oldest?"

That was a pretty simple question.

"Greg. Byron is next to me. After Byron, it's Baboo, aka Rodney. After Baboo, then Howard."

Andy nodded.

"Oh, okay."

I couldn't let the story rest there.

"I really learned a lot from my older brother, Greg. Correction. We all did. I can remember as a kid watching him and my brother Howard play in high school. They were both starters on varsity for Madison. I was the ball boy at all their games. I couldn't wait to run out there and get the ball and give it to the referee."

Andy smiled.

"My oldest brother, Greg, was one of the oldest point guards I ever saw at the time. The way he handled the ball and threw the no-look pass was unbelievable."

I smiled and corrected myself.

"Andy, let me take that back. There's one other guy I saw do it like that. That was Charlie Appleberry's little brother 'Man Man'." These guys were gym legends at the time. During that time, it didn't matter how good you were in high school. If your name wasn't ringing in the gyms or in the parks, you got no respect. You had to make your name amongst the street legends to be respected."

Andy's eyebrows raised again in surprise.

"Oh, wow. I didn't know that."

I smiled.

"In our time, I was more concerned about making a name in the parks and in the gyms. It was about being respected back then. I can remember seeing guys who started varsity for their high schools and came to the gym but wouldn't get picked to play. It was serious competition back then."

Andy wanted to know more about who was dominating the parks and the gyms. To be honest, I couldn't remember them all.

"I can't name them all, but to name a few, you had Carl Wright, Larry Johnson, Kato Armstrong, Sketta Henry, Charlie Appleberry, Charles Washington, Neil Derrick, Alfredo Porter, Steven "Hedake" Smith, Mike Mcgee, and trust me, there were many more. At Juanita Recreation Center, aka "The House of Pain," every day there was someone new that was dominating the gym that day."

He asked about Juanita Craft Recreation Center.

"It's on the East Side of Dallas, right next to the Frazier Court Projects."

I could tell that didn't mean much to him, but memories of that place flooded my mind as we talked about it.

"Is that the gym you grew up playing in?"

A big smile stretched across my face.

"Yes."

Andy nodded.

"Who were some of the guys that inspired you as you were coming up at Juanita craft?"

I chuckled. There was no simple answer to that.

"Where should I start?"

Andy laughed.

"Start anywhere you like."

I put my hand beneath my chin and let my mind go back in time to see the once-familiar faces.

"Mark Hollands, Bill, Pea Head, Fat, Billy Goat, World, Rodger Irving, Derkie, Tank, Eric, Pee Wee, Arthur Cook, Fat Fred, Drake, Mke McGee, Bee Bee, Doc, McFarland, Fred Secession, Tony Craig, J.B., and of course my brothers. Those are just to name a few. I know I missed out on many more names. Juanita Craft Recreation center was a one-of-a-kind place. You had to be tough to play in there, and I'm not just saying this to be saying it. I can remember a guy got shot 8 or 9 times over a foul ball! You had to give respect and be respected when you came to Juanita Craft. It was no joke."

Andy looked at me and his eyes were wide and round.

"Wow," was all he said before moving on to the next question. "When did it all start for you?"

I wasn't sure I understood what he meant.

"The hoop dream? When did you realize you wanted to play basketball?"

I am sure my face lit up like a Christmas tree when he asked that question. It was the one I'd been waiting to answer since he got here.

Chapter 4: Hoop Dreams

It had been years since I'd played in that neighborhood, but I could still remember the tree next door to us that served as my first basketball pole.

"The hoop dream started in a vacant lot next to the house I grew up in as a kid. We would take a bicycle rim and nail it to the tree. That was our basketball goal."

Andy shook his head in disbelief.

"Are you kidding me?"

I chuckled. It was still pretty amazing to me.

"No, I'm not. Times were rough back then. We couldn't afford a new basketball goal, let alone a new basketball. We would play with either used basketballs that people gave to us or those that we found at the park. Some days, we had to play with a flat basketball."

Andy smiled.

"Oh, wow! How did you guys manage to do that?"

I thought back to all those hours spent watching Dr. J play on television.

"It was cool for me. For some reason, as a kid, I always wanted to dunk. Especially after watching Dr. J play on television. I was notorious for running and jumping off the tree to dunk the basketball. It would be raining and muddy outside, but it didn't matter to me. All I wanted to do was play basketball. I would visualize dunking on people, emulating the moves I saw Dr. J doing on T.V. My dream was to one day play in the NBA."

I laughed as I thought about it.

"My brothers and I would practice interviewing each other as if we were already playing in the pros. In my wildest dreams, I had no idea, that one day this dream would come true and I would be in rookie camp with the Los Angeles Lakers. Back then, I didn't understand the law of attraction."

Andy nodded.

"You were definitely practicing one of the laws."

I smiled in agreement.

"You're right. If you can see it, you can be it. I can remember when I finally got a real basketball goal. I have no idea where Kerri Ann got that basketball goal from."

I hadn't thought of Kerri Ann in years, but the thought of her brings a smile to my face.

"Kerri Ann was my friend. She was light skinned, tall, and tough. She was a tom boy and just three years older than me. Their house was directly in back of our house. The only thing separating our houses was an eight-foot fence. I never saw anybody jump a fence with such precision as Kerri Ann. She was one-of-a-kind."

I shook my head as I remembered all that she'd done for me.

"She was better than any handyman in the neighborhood. She actually built a basketball goal for me from scratch. She took an old piece of plywood and nailed it to the tree, climbed up the latter, held the goal up with her head, and nailed the nails into the plywood."

Andy burst out laughing at the thought of that.

"Wow."

I chuckled and shook my head.

"Kerri Ann was something else. Her family moved to Dallas from the country. They were the Beverly Hillbillies of the neighborhood. No kidding. They actually dressed and looked like the characters that were on the television show. They were good people, though. I love Kerri Ann to this day for the things she would do for me."

Andy stopped me for a moment.

"Are you guys still friends?"

I sighed and shook my head.

"I haven't seen her since I was a kid."

Andy nodded and then shook his head. I felt as sad as he looked.

"Wow."

We sat there for a moment and then he asked his next question.

"Tell me more about the basketball games under the tree."

I shook my head as I thought about those days.

"They were competitive and physical. You would think we were playing for the NBA Finals."

I laughed at the memories.

"Elbows would be coming from everywhere. There were no rules. You had to be tough, or you weren't allowed to play. You couldn't be a cry baby. Fist fights sometimes broke out during the games."

Andy joined me in laughing.

"You guys were only kids!"

I smiled.

"I know. It wasn't only competitive under our tree. It was competitive up under every tree in the neighborhood that had a basketball goal. My friends and I would go from back yard to back yard in the neighborhood and play for bragging rights. Hamilton was a tough street to win on. The games in Gary Watson's backyard were physical and intense. Kerri Lari, may he rest in peace, was no joke with the elbows."

It seemed like a lifetime ago.

"Those guys were tough. They wanted to win, and losing wasn't an option. The same rules applied at Dunbar Park. It was war every day on that court. A potential fist fight would break out at any given time. It was survival of the fittest, and if you weren't a certain age, you weren't allowed to be on the court. Fortunately, I was an exception to the rule. I was the only youngster allowed to play with the older guys. They saw potential in me early."

I leaned forward a bit and went on with the story.

"I was taught by my brothers that if I played with older guys, my game would be advanced and I would be better than the guys my age. Fortunately, they were right."

I stopped for a moment and looked away. This part was harder to tell.

"Playing at the park was fun, but it soon came to an end. The abuse in our house took its toll and we moved in with our cousins, Jeff and Mrs. Gray. They were an older couple that lived in a three-bedroom house in Pleasant Grove. The house was over crowded, but we managed to see it through. Some nights we slept on the floor, some nights we slept in the bed. They were warm and loving people, and they made their home our home. May those two rest in peace."

I turned toward the window and quiet fell over the room as I thought about the days I spent with those two.

"How did you feel when you had to leave your friends and old neighborhood behind?"

Andy's voice broke through my reminiscing and I did my best to answer.

"It was bitter, but sweet. Leaving that abusive household was the best thing that could have happened, but leaving my friends was the worst. Some of the things we experienced when we lived with my father was unbelievable. I remember coming home late one night after attending baseball practice with my childhood friend, Dante. I didn't call to let anybody know where I was, and my father panicked."

I swallowed hard as I allowed myself to relive that awful moment.

"He was in a rage as he sat silently on that couch. 'WHERE HAVE YOU BEEN?' he roared at me in that deep voice of his as I walked through the door. I was shaking like a rattle snake, scared as heck, and the words couldn't seem to come out of my mouth. 'Take your shirt off!' His voice sounded so angry. Before I could even get my shirt over my head, I felt the welps begin to form on my body from the extension cord he was using to whip me. I screamed and hollered as I tried to escape him and flee into my mothers arms. 'Stop! You're going to kill him' her voice echoed out into the heavens as she begged him to quit. But her voice fell on deaf ears. He did not even hear her. He continued applying force as he gripped my arm tighter, stopping me from getting away."

I stopped and took a breath.

"The sweat bubbles were starting to form on his forehead. The disturbing odor of Jim Bean leaked from his pores. I screamed, 'I won't do it anymore!' He ignored me, gripped his bottom lip, and continued to apply more lashes. The look on my mother's face was indescribable. She tried her best to make me feel better after that episode. 'Your daddy loves you. I've never seen him that worried before,' she told me as she wiped the tears off my face. I wasn't buying it. I am still bothered by that episode. It doesn't sit well with me at all. I wasn't a perfect child, I stayed in trouble. I was a kid. I understand that I needed to be disciplined, but no kid deserves that kind of abuse."

Andy shook his head in disbelief.

"I agree."

He allowed me a few moments to collect myself before asking the next question.

"How long did you guys live with your cousins?"

Thinking about that freed me from the grip of the memory of that abuse.

"About a year. Then we moved to another part of Pleasant Grove, around the corner from Spruce High School. We lived 14 deep in a 3-bedroom home. Times were tough, but we managed to pull through. I don't know how we did it, but we did. At times, there was tension in the house, but for the most part it was love."

Andy's response was an amazed, "Wow."

Chapter 5: Biddie Ball

His next question was about the neighborhood.

"That area of Pleasant Grove was quiet and isolated. There weren't many places we could go and play ball until my cousin, Nikel, introduced me to Mr. Taylor and Coach Richardson. They had a little league basketball team based out of Pleasant Grove called The Dallas Trojans. Our games were played at The Salvation Army on Elm Road. I was excited to be playing there."

I grinned, recalling that first game.

"That first game with the Trojans was epic. Nikel had told Mr. Richardson and Mr. Taylor how cold I was. They told him to bring me to a basketball game so they could see what all the hype was all about. They wanted to know if I was really as good as Nikel said I was."

I shook my head and chuckled.

"I remember it as if it were yesterday. Nikel brought me to the game. It takes Hedake to tell this story. He tells it to this day! So we get to the game and, at this time, it was a twelve and under league. The goals were 8 feet. It was biddie basketball, but I didn't know what that was back then. I had been outside at the park playing when Nikel picked me up so I had on a pair of Chuck Taylor tennis shoes with no socks.

When we got to the game, they were fresh out of jerseys so I had to play in a football jersey. Mind you, everybody was waiting on me to get in that game because my cousin had been hyping me up. They finally let me in the game after half time and on the first play, I rebound the ball, take off up court, went behind my back, down the middle, and dunked. The rest is history."

I can't help but laugh at the memory of the looks on their faces.

"What's so crazy about that situation is that I didn't know I wasn't supposed to dunk. It was against the rules in biddie basketball. But that was the start of my basketball career in Pleasant Grove. I was a Trojan from that day on."

Andy laughed until he couldn't laugh anymore. I let him catch his breath and went on.

"I appreciate Coach Richardson and Mr. Taylor for all they did for me. They accepted me as one of their own, and they treated me no differently from any other guys. Those were some of the best days of my life. I looked forward to those little league games. It took my mind off what I was going through at home.

The house was overcrowded, and I was missing my friends from my old neighborhood. It was tough. There weren't many places in my new neighborhood to play basketball, so sometimes I would walk up to Spruce High School and shoot on the goals by myself to kill time. This neighborhood was boring.

I looked forward to my mother dropping my brothers and me off in East Dallas at the Mcgees's for school before she went to work. She wanted us to still be able to attend school with our friends. I thank God for the Mcgees to this day.

There was Grandmama, Granddaddy, Pete, Tammie, Big Kevin, and Kenneray Mcgee. They were there for us in our time of need. They were more than friends. They were family. We call each other cousins to this day.

I was in seventh grade at Fred F. Florence, Jr. High School. This was my first time being introduced to organized ball playing. Coach Giles was our coach. He was a beast on the court as well as off the court. This was also my first experience with discipline, outside of my father and mother.

Coach Giles would take us into his office in the gym and he would pull out his paddle and give us licks if we were disobedient in school. Everybody in the school respected Coach Giles. He used to walk around with a toothpick in his mouth. He was no joke. He was an amazing coach, one of the best coaches I've played for. We were unbeatable. We won the city championship by fifty points. Our opponents walked off the court and quit.

Florence was an amazing school. Great people, great teachers. Wouldn't trade that experience for the world."

Chapter 6: Back To The Old Neighborhood

"Fortunately, things were starting to get better around the house. Mom received her voucher from Section 8. That was a happy day for my brothers and me. We were finally going to have a place of our own and be reacquainted with our childhood friends. We packed up and moved into the Frazier Courts projects in East Dallas. Man, was I nervous."

Andy stopped me for a moment.

"Why were you nervous?"

It is tough for an outsider to understand.

"The projects were no joke back then. I didn't know what to expect. East Dallas was territorial at the time. I grew up in the houses as a kid, and the houses and the projects didn't really get along. If you lived in the houses, it wasn't a good idea to get caught in the projects and vice versa.

Also, during this time in the 80's, there was turmoil going on in the projects. There was a territorial battle happening. The North Dallas projects closed down and merged into the East Dallas projects. This was a disaster waiting to happen. They fought constantly. They were at war strong for about two years or more. It was tough.

I can remember playing on the basketball court and the guys from the North Dallas projects had to watch their backs constantly. Fights would break out rapidly."

Andy adjusted his notepad on the table and resumed the interview with a perplexed look on his face.

"Wow. Weren't you afraid?"

I shrugged.

"At times, but we were originally from East Dallas, so we had no problems. We were familiar with a lot of the guys from school and the gym."

Andy wanted to know more.

"Why were they beefing over territorial rights?"

My answer was simple.

"One reason was drugs. Crack was on the rise. A lot of money was starting to be accumulated from this drug. Other drugs were selling as well, but they weren't bringing in the big bucks like crack cocaine. So, sharing the same block was non-negotiable.

Another reason was that new people weren't allowed in the neighborhood. Fortunately, as time moved on, things got better. The guys started to get along. I would have to credit the gym for that. The more we played at Juanita Craft Recreation Center, also known as the house of pain, the more the guys acquired a mutual respect for each other."

Andy wanted to talk about the gym.

"What were the games like at Juanita Craft during that time?"

I sat back with a smile and thought about those days. I could still hear the squeak of sneakers on those floorboards.

"They were competitive. You had to have a heart to play in the house of pain. The competition was so fierce that if you didn't get to the gym early, your chances of playing that day were slim. There were three courts to play on and each one of them would be occupied at all times. The two courts on the sides were for the little boys, and the middle one was for the big boys."

I chuckled just thinking about it.

"Once you were allowed to play on the middle court, you were official. You'd finally arrived. The competition was fierce on that middle court. The older guys were advanced. They were fundamentally sound. I can remember sitting back, watching these guys play. It was a sight to see.

They were doing things on the court that were unheard of in pick up ball. They were picking and rolling and blocking out. To be honest, I never saw anybody set a pick like Tank. He was known for his picks. If you weren't ready, you were going down. They were truly advanced players. You had to have fundamentals to play out there with those guys. If you missed Bill's pass as he came off the pick and roll, you were doomed for ridicule."

I shook my head, remembering those days.

"Nobody wanted to win as much as Mark Holland. Nobody took control over the game like Charlie Appleberry. Nobody threw the no look pass like Harold Sanders. Nobody attacked the basketball goal with the tenacity of Billy Goat. Watching and play with these guys every day advanced my game. The competition in school was tough, but the competition in that gym was tougher. Many fights broke out at Juanita Craft Recreation Center. Many guns were pulled out. A guy got shot 9 times arguing with another guy over a foul ball."

Andy could not believe it.

"Wow!!"

I nodded. It was pretty intense, although it seemed normal to me back then because that was all I knew.

"The craft was rough, as well as the neighborhood. The drug scene was on the rise. Money was starting to circulate throughout the community. Crack was on the rise. Fortunately, I was protected from a lot of the riffraff. Being an athlete in the hood came with privileges. Normally, the bad actors would give you a pass. They wouldn't bother with you. Actually, some would go so far as to protect you. They wanted you to make it out. There were good people and fun times in the neighborhood.

The jams in the park were off the chain. Earth Quake, the former D.J. of Vanilla Ice, would bring his turn tables out and play music in the back of the gym. He would bring all the projects out. The park would be lit. The barbecue grills would be smoking. The Nissan trucks and slant back Sevilles would be pulling up. Guys would be walking their pit bulls. There was no pit bull in the neighborhood like Moe. He was the first pit bull I ever saw run up a tree and lock its jaws on a tree branch. That dog gave us a show. He was the first celebrity dog from the hood."

Andy laughed.

"Really?"

I grinned. The image of that dog swinging from that tree branch came to mind.

"Yes, he was a sight to see. I had some good times living in the projects. Until one day, I came home from school and found out some devastating news. I remember it like it was yesterday. It was the day before school let out. I was in the 8th grade at Florence Middle School. It was weird, because that day all the teachers arrived late. They were talking about a bad accident that had traffic backed up that morning. That day after school, my childhood friend, Paul, walked home with me. Something felt strange when we walked in the door.

Eric Brooks, my childhood friend, and my brother, Byron, were sitting at the kitchen table in complete silence. When I looked out the window, I could see my father's van parked out back. I thought that was strange because my father and I spoke on the phone the day before and it went all bad after he and my mother exchanged words.

I turned and looked at my mother. 'Where is my daddy?' She looked back at me and said, 'Your father is dead. He was killed in a car wreck.'

After I heard the news, I ran in the room next to the staircase and bawled. That was a tough day for me. My father was dead, and I never got the chance to know him. Shortly after his death, we were awarded the house on Metropolitan that we grew up in, so we left the projects and headed back to our old neighborhood.

We were back home, finally. The heat was scorching, and the summer months were taking their toll. The summer was coming to an end. I had to make a decision on which high school I wanted to go to. Byron decided to enroll part-time in the business magnet downtown, so that's where my childhood friend, T.I.P., and I decided to enroll, too.

Our home school was Madison, and TIP's was Samuel. To be honest, TIP and I went for the women, and Byron actually went for the education. TIP and I would skip school with the girls and take them back to our house. Since we were downtown near the bus line, it was easy access. Some mornings, before school, we would walk over to the Arts Magnet to see our friends, Tam, Che-Che, and Apples. Apples was also known as Erykah Badu. Tam was my chick at the time.

Sometimes, I wonder what it would have been like if Tam and I had stayed together. She was a real one, and we shared some special times. We all pretty much lived in the same area. We lived on one side of the neighborhood, and they lived on the other. They were truly talented young ladies. They could sing like no one else. Tam was singing in night clubs in high school. Whoever thought they would one day get record deals? Not that I ever doubted them. It was just amazing to see, because they all came from humble beginnings."

Andy nodded.

"Nice. Could you elaborate on what part-time means?"

I was happy to explain.

"Part-time is when a student attends a magnet school for half of the day and their home school the other half. You had the best of both worlds. You had an option to attend in the AM or the PM. We chose to attend in the AM. The magnet school consisted of a cluster, which is similar to taking up a trade. For example, if you wanted to study business, you attended the business magnet. If you wanted to be an artist, you attended the arts magnet, and so on."

"Oh, really?" Andy said. "What was Madison like?"

I thought about the best way to answer that question.

"Madison was no joke. It was a modern day Lean On Me. Man, if you were soft, you weren't going to make it. There were instances where people got their lunches taken, and they didn't resist. I remember being in Ms. Shelly's class 7th period. It was located on the 3rd floor, next to the stair case. We heard a gunshot and looked out the window.

We saw a guy running a hundred miles an hour across the back lawn. He'd been shot. He had an altercation with a guy at the bottom of the steps over a dice game. I was told that he ran all the way over to the graveyard on Spring and Oakland before he realized that the bullet only scraped his head.

Besides that, for the most part, Madison was cool. Pretty much my entire family graduated from Madison. Madison showed me love."

Andy stopped me again.

"Why didn't you play basketball there?"

I laughed.

"That's a long story. I decided that if I wasn't going to play varsity, I wasn't going to play at all. It came off as arrogance at the time, but I didn't see it that way. I saw it as confidence."

Andy nodded.

"What happened?"

I shook my head.

"I went to Coach Kid, the Head Basketball Coach at the time, and asked him if I could try out for varsity."

Andy leaned forward.

"What did he say?"

I shrugged.

"He didn't say anything. He gave me the funniest look you could give someone and walked away."

Andy waited for me to continue.

"What happened after that?"

I smiled.

"I walked away. I stuck to the decision I'd made that if I wasn't going to play varsity, I wasn't going to play at all, and I sat my freshman year out."

Andy's face registered his surprise.

"Really?"

I shifted in my seat a bit.

"Yes. It was a tough decision for me at the time. All my brothers played for Coach Kidd, and I wanted to follow in their footsteps, but Spruce was a better look for me at the time. Ironically, I approached Coach Rhodes my freshman year also."

Andy prompted me to continue sharing the story.

"Really?"

I let my mind drift backward to that year.

"My cousin, Nikel, took me to Spruce High School to meet Coach Rhodes. He was the head basketball coach at the time. He also taught chemistry."

Andy wanted more details.

"What happened?

I smiled as I remembered those days.

"We went to his classroom and waited for him to come out. It took a while. When he finally came out, he was this 6'7" light-skinned, curly haired man with this look on his face that would intimidate the masses. He gazed at the both of us and said, 'What do y'all want?' Nikel said, 'This is my cousin, Ike. He would like to try out for varsity.' He looked at both of us and walked back into the classroom. It was hilarious.

From that moment on, I had something to prove. Every day I trained. Every night I worked on my game at the park, with no lights. I was told by Greg, my older brother, that if you could make a shot in the dark, think how many you would make when the lights were on. I was relentless. He gave me a weight jacket and leg weights. I wore them when I ran the stairs in the back of Dunbar elementary. I was determined to prove my point.

A wise man once said, 'When the competition is asleep, you gotta be working. You have to go twice as hard as the next man.' I was pumped. I remember running across Fitzhugh Bridge with that weight jacket on, not knowing if I was going to make it the next five yards. But I kept going. I didn't quit. I was determined to make a statement when my opportunity came."

Chapter 7: Opportunity Arrives

"Did your opportunity ever come?"

Andy's question made me smile.

"Yeah, thanks to Mr. Richardson, my Little League coach. He familiarized Coach Rhodes with who I was, so Coach Rhodes decided to give me a shot at varsity. I enrolled in Spruce my sophomore year. I was still attending business magnet part-time. I was anxious. I couldn't wait for 7th period athletics. This was my opportunity to prove myself. When 7th period finally arrived, the gym was hot and sticky. People were everywhere. The talent at Spruce was fierce.

Hedake and his freshmen team were on the rise. He, and some of his teammates, would be moving up to varsity. The tryouts were going to be tough. There was no room for mistakes. The scrimmages were intense as I watched from the side line, awaiting my opportunity. Finally, Coach Rhodes looked at me and said, 'Son, go in.' After that scrimmage, Coach Rhodes was convinced.

He pulled me to the side and said, 'Son, you are going to be my starting two guard on varsity.' And the rest was history."

I couldn't help but laugh at the memory of that triumph. Andy smiled and laughed along with me before asking the next question.

"What was it like playing for Coach Rhodes?"

That was a great question.

"It was a great experience. He was a man of principles and values, and he instilled those things in his players as well. He stood for something, both on and off of the court. He was a young coach that was under a lot of pressure at that time. He had a lot of talent and he had to find a way to make everybody happy and win.

That task wasn't easy. How do you tell a senior guard that he would not be starting that year, that you were going to go with this sophomore who just popped up out of nowhere. It was hard for him, and for me. We both dealt with issues on and off the court from outside sources.

At times, it felt like some of the decisions that he made on the court were based off of that. I couldn't understand it then, but now, as a man, I do. It was an honor to play for him. He gave me an opportunity when nobody else would.

I needed Coach Rhodes in my life at that time, because I was starting to spiral out of control off the court. I needed the discipline he imparted to us. He was that father figure I didn't have at home. He helped make that bridge easier for me to cross. I'm grateful for him to this day because of that."

Andy stared at me silently. Then, he smiled.

"Now that Coach Rhodes finally let you have that opportunity, did you make a statement?"

I crossed my arms in front of my chest and leaned back.

"Yes, I did. I remember it as if it were yesterday. It was my sophomore year, my first game on varsity. We were playing Dallas Kimball in our home gym. I was as nervous as a harlot in a church. It was standing room only. The crowd was intense. People came from everywhere to see what the hype was all about. They wanted to know if Hedake and Ike-Moe were really as good as people said we were.

The pressure was on. I remember getting a fast break. I was thinking this could make me or break me as I dribbled the ball down the court. Before I knew it, I cupped the ball in my right hand, took off, and slam dunked. I did it 2 more times after that.

The crowd went ballistic. The adrenaline rush was indescribable. It was a feeling I'd never experienced before, and I was hooked like a kid on sweets. My childhood dream finally came true. I became known for my vicious slam dunk.

As a child, all I dreamed about was dunking. I remember going from door to door in the house with two socks balled up into one, visualizing myself dunking on someone. My momma used to holler through the house, 'Boy, quit that jumping in there!' I had no idea that sock would one day turn into a basketball. The hard work was finally starting to pay off.

The long nights at the parks were starting to make sense. I can still feel the pain in my legs from running up and down those stairs in back of Dunbar school. I remember being at the park at night and having to make 100 free throws in the dark before I went home. It was tough, but it was all worth it. I have no regrets. The hard work paid off. I became sophomore of the year both in all-area and in all-region that year. I was starting to gain notoriety in the city.

The girls were starting to pay attention. I met my soon-to-be son's mother. I was in love at first sight. Things were finally starting to make sense. I had one of the finest chicks in the city, and my name was starting to ring like a school bell.

I used to love it in the morning at business magnet when the principal would acknowledge me on the intercom. He would mention how many points I scored in the game the night before with the morning announcements. Now, mind you, none of the magnet schools had sports. For Mr. Walker to acknowledge me was big.

Chapter 8: The Shift (Becoming Intrigued By the Streets)

"Now I'm starting to attract the attention of the city. People are starting to recognize me. I'm becoming a neighborhood superstar, attracting the attention of the neighborhood hustlers and drug dealers. I was intrigued by their lifestyle, their fancy clothes, their exotic cars, and how the women took to them.

That excited me. I watched guys with whom I played basketball in the park become millionaires in the dope gang. They were neighborhood kingpins. When crack came to the neighborhood, things went from moderate to extreme. Everything changed. People who never had money before had money. People started getting killed. Families were being destroyed. Friends I played ball with every day were going away to jail for a long time.

I watched crack destroy my whole neighborhood. My attitude started to change. I no longer lived in a friendly zone anymore. Those days were over. The friends I once hung out with on the park benches were now on the corner selling crack. I was fortunate. I had a mother that didn't go for that and friends that wanted to see me make it out.

They gave me the things I wanted to ensure that I wouldn't get in the game. They wouldn't let me hustle, even if I wanted to. I was their hope, and I didn't want to let them down. I remember being at the park shooting ball by myself when one of Dallas's first drug kingpins, Anthony Ray King, walked through the park.

He had two of his body guards walking beside him. He walked in the middle with a full length black fur coat tucked over his shoulders. He said to me as he passed, 'I'm coming to see you tomorrow. You better do something.' That meant something to me at the time. I knew what he said was genuine. We all played basketball in the park together before he became as big as he was in the drug game.

I can remember cursing him out when he missed my no look pass. He was physical and a good rebounder. His nickname was Rat. May he rest in peace. We had love in the neighborhood at the time. Where ever I played, my neighborhood would be there.

After the game, World would make sure I was ok. He was connected to Anthony Ray in the drug game. I watched Anthony Ray and him count so much money at Kiest Park, it scared me to death. But for some reason, I was intrigued by what I was seeing.

I can remember walking home from the gym and Foreman Street would be crowded with traffic. The drug game was in full effect. I would be nervous walking through there. At any given time, something could pop off. I had to show respect, because some of these guys were my biggest supporters, ensuring nothing happened to me. The love was unexplainable."

Chapter 9: Gaining Recognition

"That love kept me motivated to become the best ball player I could. So I went back to the drawing board. More jump shots, more stairs. My recognition was continuing to grow. I was asked to play AAU basketball. This was big for me at the time. I was finally becoming recognized. Headake was our point guard. His name was starting to ring out as well. Our chemistry was unexplainable.

He was becoming a sophomore, and I was becoming a junior. We took summer league by surprise. The things we did on the court, for some reason, people wouldn't let go. I can't explain it. I guess it was magic. Then school started back up, and summer was over. The hype on Spruce was getting bigger. We were getting exposure from the local newspapers.

At that time, if you made the paper you was somebody. There was no internet at that time. Making the news was unheard of, but we were loaded with talent. Lesley Booker, Derrick Richardson, Tondrell Durham, Kelvin "Manute" Chambers, Headake, Quinton Bass and more. All eyes were on Spruce, but my eyes were on ten 5A. Our district was loaded with talent.

Larry Johnson was at Skyline. Alfredo Porter and Snake were at SOC. Neil Derrick was at Garland. Tim Fleming, Ray Shufford, and Big Gentry were at Kimball. The list went on and on. Every night, you had to come to play. Every district, from 4A to 5A, was loaded with talent. The talent was that fierce and the competition started to become tougher. I was now on the coach's radar. I was no longer a surprise.

College scouts were coming to watch us play. We started the season off with a bang. Every game was standing room only. If you weren't there before 6 or 6:30, you weren't getting in."

Andy broke through my reminiscing for the briefest of moments with a characteristic, "Wow!!"

I nodded and grinned. It was pretty amazing.

"We were becoming a force to be reckoned with. Everybody wanted to beat us, and we didn't take that challenge lightly. We had a great season. We made it all the way to the second round in the play offs. Unfortunately, we lost, but I had a good season. I was named first team all-area, first team all-region, and second team all-state.

Recruiting letters from major colleges started to come in by the ship loads, as did the women. And, with the women, came the drinking and partying. I was starting to have more sex than I ever had before. I was participating in ménage à trois and orgies with different women. I was doing well on the court, but I was starting to spiral out-of-control off the court.

I was becoming a product of my environment. For some reason, I wanted to be part of the street culture. My best friend, George, and I would ride around with guns. He had a sawed-off shotgun and I had a .38.

I met George Green my sophomore year at Spruce. We clicked at first site. He was about 6'2", with a wide body. He was a force to be reckoned with on the basketball court. He was our starting forward, and my best friend. We had a lot in common. We both liked the women, and we both were intrigued by the streets. We were partners in crime.

We were together every day. His father took me in as if I were his on son. I loved Pops. He was a kool old cat, the father I never had. I admired the relationship between George and him. He would let us cruise around in his blue El Dog. That was one of the cleanest caddies I ever rode in.

George made the transition to Spruce easy for me. His friends became my friends. The OG' s in Pleasant Grove loved him like the OG' s in East Dallas loved me. They would gave us anything we wanted. They took good care of us. They gave us money, cars to drive, and anything else we wanted. In their eyes, we were solid young dudes."

Andy's mouth dropped open in amazement.

"Wow!! You were spiraling out of control, and no one ever knew."

I nodded my head in agreement.

"You're right. No one never knew because my appearance and my performance on the court never reflected what was really going on in my life. Thanks to basketball, it kept me from going over the edge, and falling overboard into the streets."

Andy shook his head in disbelief.

"You're very fortunate. What was your senior season at Spruce like?"

Those were some amazing times.

"Spruce was now officially a household name for basketball. We had Headake at the point, I was at two, Tondrell Durham was at three, George Green was at the four, and Mike Williams was at the five. We kicked butt.

We made it to the Championship game in the Dr. Pepper Tournament, where I was named MVP. I was the first player in the history of the Dr. Pepper tournament to lose in the Championship game and still be named MVP."

Andy shook his head in amazement.

"That's unbelievable!"

I couldn't have said it better.

"It was. We had an awesome season and made it all the way to the reginal semi-finals. Unfortunately, we lost. I was later named 1st Team All Area, 1st Team All Region, 1st Team All State, and Honorable Mention All American."

Chapter 10: Proposition 48

Now that my senior season had come to a close, it was time to pick a college and take the SAT/ACT. Picking a college was cool, but taking the SAT/ACT was a nightmare.

Andy leaned forward in his seat.

"How many college visits did you make?"

That was a long time ago, but it wasn't hard for me to remember. Each campus represented a new possibility for my life.

"I visited Texas, Baylor, Houston, Odessa Junior College, and New Mexico, of course, but a lot of the other colleges that were recruiting me were afraid to take a chance. They wanted to see if I was going to have the test scores first."

He listened patiently and then asked, "What were some of the other colleges that were recruiting you at the time?"

"All of the Big East, Sec, Pac 10, and many other conferences. All I had to do was pass my test and I was on my way."

He looked puzzled. I'm sure that test was no big deal to a man like him, but it had been a very big deal to me back then.

"Why did you feel the SAT/ACT was a nightmare?"

I thought about the sweat on the palm of my hands as I sat in those hard chairs in those cold rooms gripping that number 2 pencil and took those tests. Every bubble represented a piece of my future that might be slipping away.

"These tests were new. Many school districts didn't know how to prepare the students to take them. The suburban communities had better programs in place, but the inner-city schools suffered. These tests were an athlete's nightmare. Many athletes failed the tests and had to go to junior college, or become a proposition 48.

Proposition 48 allowed an athlete to attend university, but you weren't allowed to play your freshman year. Unfortunately, I was a proposition 48 at the University of New Mexico. This was one of the hardest things I had to do physically and mentally."

He leaned back on his stool. "Why do you say that?"

The bitter disappointment I'd felt when I received my results was nothing compared to living with the consequences.

"My momentum was broken. Having to sit out my freshman year at New Mexico was tough, not just for me, but for my roommate Khari Jaxon, too. He was also a proposition 48. We were both 18 or 19 years old at the time. It was our first time away from home and in an unfamiliar city. It was tough.

I broke out with hives on my legs and my nerves were bad. It was a culture shock. This was my first time being around so many different cultures, and I had a hard time adjusting. I just wanted to go home. I packed my bags up, called the coaches, and told them I was leaving never to return."

Andy nodded as he took some notes.

"Did you leave?"

I shook my head.

"No. I stayed. Going back home wouldn't have been a good idea. Things were really getting bad there. The gang culture was on the rise. The dope dealers were fighting against the Jamaicans over drug territory. It wouldn't have been wise to go back, so I stayed. I did whatever I had to do to get adjusted.

Things gradually started getting better. Khari and I would play basketball every day at Johnson Center with the team, and sometimes at the PIT before team practices. We weren't allowed to practice with the team because of the proposition rules and regulations."

Andy looked up. "That had to be tough."

He had no idea.

"Sure it was. It was humiliating, as well as frustrating. I felt like people thought I was dumb and incompetent. We sat on the bench with the team at every home game, but we couldn't dress out. We stood out like giants amongst midgets, which made things even more frustrating.

That frustration, among many other things, led me into partying, women, and excessive drinking. I was slipping into the darkness. I was suffering from situational depression and I needed solutions fast! I looked forward to the holidays when we were allowed to go home and visit our families.

I had a blast when I went back home. My family and friends were excited to see me, and so were the neighborhood hustlers. Something about that lifestyle intrigued me. I wasn't sure if it was the fancy cars and the jewelry, the 100 spoke Dayton rims and the Trues and Vogues tires the old school Cadillacs were riding on, or the big bank rolls that were in the guy's pockets. I don't know, but there was something that just couldn't keep me away from hanging out with these guys until I experienced one of the biggest scares of my life."

Chapter 11: The Scare

"What was it?" Andy wanted to know.

I paused for a moment to collect my thoughts before I answered.

"My brother got shot during Christmas break."

Andy's eyebrows raised and his eyes got round. I am sure that's not what he expected to hear.

"Me and my brother, Baboo, and one of the top dope dealers from the neighborhood were at a night club in Dallas off of Greenville Avenue. During those times, Nissan trucks with Dayton wire spokes were the vehicles to have. My friend had a white one with 100 spoke Daytons, all chrome.

After the club, we were all standing out in front of my friend's truck, talking to the girls, and a guy dropped a 40-ounce beer. It spilled on his tires.

'What did he do that for?' I said, shaking my head.

All hell broke loose. My friend and the guy started arguing back and forth. I was talking to a girl I knew from high school and heard all of the commotion, so I turned around to see what was happening. My friend was on the cell phone talking to a female in the truck when his door opened, and I saw two guys approaching him.

My brother was near me, so we both approached the truck to see what the problem was. These two guys wouldn't stop arguing. Luckily, a friend from high school walked up. We recognized each other and tried to diffuse the situation. These guys were his little cousins. Before I knew it, one of the guys snatched the phone out of my friend's hand. At that point, we had to defend ourselves.

I hit one guy and my brother hit the other guy. The guy I hit got up and went to a car nearby and came back shooting. He shot my friend in the side and knocked him back into the truck. Then he came around, aiming to shoot me in the head, but I slipped down due to the shoes I was wearing. He shot and hit my brother in the leg, instead. Thank God he didn't finish the job."

"What happened next?" Andy asked.

I could hear the nervousness in his voice. It was nothing compared to the nervousness I'd felt after my brother was shot.

"I got up and grabbed my brother, put him in the car, and flew to the hospital. He was in pain. The bullet was burning inside his leg."

Andy kept digging.

What happened to your friend?"

I shook my head in awe of the blessings we'd all received that night.

"He made it to the hospital shortly after us. A couple of weeks later, they both recovered."

Andy put down his pen for a moment.

"Wow. That was quite a scare."

This was an understatement.

"You're right. It was by the grace of God we all lived that night. A couple of weeks later, I flew back to school. Christmas break was over. It was back to the drawing board.

Basketball season was coming to an end. Khari and I were getting closer to becoming officially a Lobo. Things were good, but for some reason trouble seemed to follow us."

Andy stopped me.

"What do you mean?"

I took a breath and continued the story.

"Khari and I and a couple of friends got into a fight in the Coronado Dorms. It was four of us against two hallways on the first floor. We were ambushed. My friend, Mark, ended up having to go to the hospital."

Andy raised an eyebrow as if he couldn't quite believe this.

"What happened to cause this event?"

That was a long story.

"Khari and I lived on the second floor in the Coronado dorms. Mark lived in the dorm next to ours. Terrance lived off campus. One night, we were all hanging out in the room, drinking and playing music. We were waiting on Newton to come pick us up. Newton was a forward on the 1989 team with Luc Longley.

Instead of waiting on Newton upstairs, we decided to wait on him in front of the dorms. While we were waiting on Newton, we were loudly discussing who was the best rapper. As we were talking, we heard a voice scream out of the window, 'Shut up, Nigggger!' At least, we thought we heard that.

So we stampeded into the dorms and started hitting and fighting everybody we saw. That wasn't a good idea, because guys were coming from everywhere, attacking us.

We were in big trouble. We were on the verge of being kicked out of school. It's a good thing they decided to put us on school probation, instead of taking harsh action. This incident made USA Today!"

Andy shook his head. "Wow!!"

It was a tough year.

"All that frustration from not being able to play was being released in all the wrong ways."

Chapter 12: Back On The Team

"Fortunately, we made it through the storm. Basketball season was over. Khari and I were back on the team. Now that the semester had come to an end, it was time to go back home and get ready for summer league at Red Bird Gym.

I was ready. I had something to prove. I'd had to sit out a year. Therefore, I had to show the people I hadn't missed a step. I was back to devour anybody that got in my way. It wasn't an easy job.

Red Bird was loaded with talent. At any given day, you could get your hat brought to you if you were slipping in your game. I knew I couldn't slip. I couldn't afford it. Missing a year of college can be hard on your reputation. People have a tendency to forget about you. I wasn't having that."

I broke out laughing, remembering those days.

"I finished summer league with a bang. My name was starting to resurface throughout the city again. I said to myself, 'Now, I have to go and take the Western Athletic Conference by storm.' So the month before I went back to New Mexico, I went back to the drawing board.

I did more late night working out, when I could. The gangs made it hard for me to work out at night, though. It wasn't safe in the neighborhood anymore. People were getting murdered. There were drive-by shootings every night. The neighborhood was insane.

I remember sitting on the park benches talking to a guy. He walked off, headed towards the corner store, never to be seen again. He was murdered. His brains were scattered all over the parking lot."

Andy gasped.

"Are you serious?"

I closed my eyes, trying to blot out the image of that night that came to mind.

"Yes, I am. It was the worst thing I ever saw in my life."

Andy hesitated, then asked, "Were you ever part of the gang culture?"

I was glad to be able to answer him honestly.

"Never. The gang culture came about when I was in college. Unfortunately, the guys a few years younger than me got caught up in it. The neighborhood was changing at a rapid rate. It was no longer a peaceful place to live. I wanted out. I couldn't wait to get back to New Mexico. I jumped on the first plane smoking.

Once I got back to Albuquerque, I felt refreshed. I was excited. I put the past behind me, and got focused. No more Proposition 48. I was finally going to get my opportunity to play in the PIT. I was looking forward to playing with Luc Longley and having my first winning season. But I wasn't prepared for the politics of the game. I didn't realize how much more learning I had to do.

I anticipated being a starter and playing multiple minutes. That wasn't so. Actually, it was the opposite. I wasn't a starter. I played less minutes."

Andy looked up again.

"That had to be tough on you mentally."

I nodded.

"It was. Until my big break came in the middle of the season, when our point guard failed to handle the pressure of New Mexico State. He was no longer trusted in the point guard position, and after the game, I was approached by the coaching staff.

They asked me, 'Do you think you can handle the point guard position?'

I didn't hesitate. 'Yes.'

I knew this would be my only chance to get some playing time.

Playing in front of our shooting guard, Rob Robbins, wasn't going to happen."

Andy prompted me for more details.

"What happened next?"

I chuckled.

"Once we got back to practice the following week, they worked me out at the point. The rest was history. I led my team to the first found in the NCAA tournament."

Andy's smile stretched across his face.

"Awesome!! What was it like playing with Luc Longley?"

This was a great question.

"Luc was a nice guy. He gave me some good advice before he left New Mexico."

Andy's face lit up.

"Really?"

I settled in to tell him the story.

"It was amazing how it happened. We had just played Wyoming and were on the charter bus headed back to Denver. It was pitch dark, with snow flurries everywhere. Everybody on the bus was asleep. I felt somebody tough me on the shoulder and tell me to come to the back. It was Luc.

He sat me down and told me to be patient. He told me my time would come and that I had to do what it took to get to the next level."

Andy looked at me.

"What did he mean when he said the next level?"

I was glad he'd asked.

"He was referring to the NBA."

Andy was impressed.

"That was good advice coming from an NBA lottery pick."

His smile was infectious and I returned it.

"What was it like playing the NCAA tournament?"

I shook my head, thinking about the excitement of those times.

"It was crazy. The energy was off the chain and the pressure was on. We were playing on NBC, and I knew I had to perform. It was a great experience. Unfortunately, we lost to Oklahoma State in the first round.

After the game, I remember going to Luc's room. Agents were everywhere. They were celebrating and drinking. It was a crazy sight to see, and I knew at that point the work I had to do. I was motivated. I wanted to feel that feeling one day.

Now that the season was over, it was back to the drawing board. I had a good season, but I was playing out of position. I wasn't a point guard. I was a two guard. I was determined to come back the following year to prove that. So, I went back home and worked hard despite what was going on around me in my community.

I stayed focused and worked on my game every day. I had a good summer league, but it wasn't good enough. I wasn't getting the respect out there I deserved. I went back to New Mexico to prove a point. The season started off good, but something was still missing.

I wasn't consistent. I would have a good game one night and the next I would suck. I couldn't get it together. I would start the game off, but I would never be in the game to the end of it. I became frustrated and lost focus. My mind was all over the place.

My high school sweetheart was pregnant with my son, Isaac. I was pledging Omega Psi Phi Fraternity at that same time. I had to get it together and quickly. Time wasn't on my side. Things were looking downhill until I had two break out games back-to-back.

It was beautiful. I can remember it like it was yesterday. We were playing Texas A&M in College Station. My family came in two vans to see me play. This one was special. This was the first time my grandmother and cousin, Yolanda, ever saw me play. I had 31 points and broke a school record for the most 3 pointers in one game."

Andy could appreciate that.

"Wow!! That was special."

I took a moment to appreciate the memory.

"It was beautiful. The next game was against Arizona State, two days before Christmas, on ESPN. The PIT was rocking.

This was the first time I played on the opposite team of my high school point guard Stephen "Hedake" Smith. This game was huge. The whole city of Dallas was tuned in to see it. There was nothing we could do with Headake. He was a general out there that night.

The game went down to the wire. They beat us on a buzzer beater. Jamal Falkner threw the ball up at the last minute. Swish! All net!"

Andy raised up from his stool in excitement.

"No!!""

I smiled.

"Yes!! It was bitter but sweet. I finished with 30 points that night. After the game, I rushed back to my apartment and packed my bags to jump on a flight back to Dallas. My high school sweetheart was in labor with my son. I made it to the hospital 10 minutes too late to see my son, Isaac Williams the Fourth, come into the world.

Chapter 13: The Pressure

"Now, the pressure was on. There was no more time for play. I had a son to provide for. Unfortunately, after those two games, my performance went back to normal. I couldn't get the momentum back until we played Virginia in the NIT Tournament. We were facing Bryan Stitt.

He was a lottery pick that year. After the game, he hugged me and gave me my respect because I didn't back down from him. That moment was inspirational for me. It let me know I had the potential to be a star if I focused. And that, I did.

I approached my senior year with a different mentality. I went back to Dallas and worked out in a way that I'd never done before. I stopped drinking and partying. I changed my diet and it paid off. I was taking summer league by storm. I had to redeem myself. My stock was going down. I wasn't holding up to my reputation.

My college performance was good, but it wasn't great. I had a point to prove. My mission was to destroy my opponent. Anybody who got in my way that summer at Red Bird, I devoured them. I took no prisoners. I had to regain my respect. It was a must."

Andy understood. "You were on a mission."

He was exactly right.

"I was. My strategy worked. My name started to ring again. One day, after summer league, I was in the bathroom. I saw a hand reach over the stall with a card in it. When I came out of the stall, he was gone. I read the card. It was Larry Johnson's agent. I felt really good at that moment. The hard work was paying off."

"Did you call him?" Andy asked.

I grinned.

"Sure, I did. He invited me to meet Larry Johnson. Larry was hosting his camp at Beckley Recreation in Oak Cliff. Little did he know, I already knew Larry."

I laughed at the thought of it.

"We grew up around the same area. We worked out together a

couple of times."

Andy joined in.

"What was Larry's reaction when he saw you?"

I shook my head.

"He was excited. It had been awhile since we saw each other. He told me I was good and I didn't have to worry about anything anymore. When I came to the camp, I didn't have to work. He wanted me to go with him and Slim every day and work out. I was excited. This was my chance to reinvent myself. I was putting my past behind me. No more wilding it out. I was a new person. I was determined and focused."

Andy wanted to know what happened next.

"I went home and got regrouped. The next morning, I headed out to camp. There I saw Jimmy King, Jason Sassar, Hedake, and more. We were all working the camp.

Every day after the kids left, we would scrimmage each other. I couldn't wait. This was my opportunity to showcase my skills. The games were intense. The gym was filled with guys like Larry Johnson, Mark Aguirre, and many other NBA players. I was the element of surprise, and I loved it.

These guys heard of me, but they didn't take me seriously. I remember watching Mark Aguirre dominate the court. He was elbowing the guys and having his way with them while I waited anxiously on the side line. I couldn't wait to play.

Finally, I got a chance to get on the court and matched up with Mark. Before the game started, he pulled his shorts up, trying to intimidate me. He had no idea what I was thinking in my head. I was hungry, and I was there to prove a point. I knew if I stood up to Mark, they had to respect me. Nobody in there knew what I could do except Larry, J, Sass, and Hedake.

The game started and Mark took me straight down low and got physical with me. Everybody was waiting to see how I was going to respond. I kept my cool. I came down court and went straight at Mark, shook him, and pulled up for the jumper, straight net.

He came back down and showed me why he was an NBA All-Star. He was the real deal. He respected me because I didn't back down. After playing against Mark, my confidence sky rocketed. I knew if I could play against Mark, I could play against anybody. Exposure is everything. The better the competition, the better the player."

Andy nodded. "That is so true. What happened next?"

Chapter 14: Politics As Usual

"After we played I went home, and got ready for the next day. When I arrived at camp that morning, I was feeling good. The respect was there, and I couldn't wait until the kids went home. I was ready to play, but something didn't feel right. I thought I was going to go work out with Larry and Slim. Slim was Larry's trainer at the time.

All of a sudden, things changed. I wondered what happened. I came to find out that there was a meeting held about me when I left the day before. I was told by a reliable source that questions were asked about me. They wanted to know if I was still wilding out and drinking."

Andy stopped me.

"You weren't drinking anymore."

I nodded my head.

"Right. I was told by a reliable source that it was during that meeting a person, whom I really respected and looked at like a brother, didn't vouch for me. They took his word as bond. The deal I had with Larry and slim fell through.

I respect Mark and Slim for standing up for me. They said, 'If ya'll won't take him, we will.' And they did just that. From then on, I was working out with Mark every day and Slim was training me. I was devastated by the news. That was the start of the politics and betrayal in my career."

Andy shook his head.

"That's tough."

I shrugged. I didn't like to dwell on it too much.

"I didn't let it break me. It was a blessing in disguise. Mark treated me like a little brother. I trained with him for the rest of the summer, and we hung out after we worked out. He took me to his house.

Mark was a cool dude. I remember riding around with him in his convertible 2-door red 500 SL. It was a sight to see."

I shook my head and laughed.

Andy made a few more notes on the notepad.

"That's cool. That was nice of Mark and Slim to take you in. What was Slim's full name?"

I will never forget that name.

"Ken Roberson."

After satisfying Andy's curiosity I continued the story.

"After working out with Slim and Mark a full summer, I was trained and ready for my senior season at New Mexico. After matching up every day with the defensive player of the year in the Big Ten, Jimmy King, I couldn't be stopped."

Chapter 15: Change

"The day I touched back down in Albuquerque, New Mexico, I was in shape and focused. In pre-season conditioning, I was no longer the guy dragging in last on the seven-minute mile. I was now at the front of the line with J.J. Griego. I went to sleep every night before eleven. I no longer ate red meat or pork. I stopped drinking alcohol. I cooled out on the partying and the women.

It was all on the line. It was my last year. I was determined to have a good season, and I did. We finished 24-7 and fifth seed in the NCAA tournament.

I was named MVP of the Lobo classic and Western Athletic Conference tournament. I led the conference in 3 point percentages. I was named first team All-WAC and first team All-Region."

Andy made a few notes. "You had a big year."

That was one way of putting it.

"I did. It was crazy!! The last 10-15 games of the season, I averaged 24 plus points a game. I was in the zone. NBA scouts were at every game. It was indescribable. The city was going nuts over the Lobos. We couldn't walk through the malls without getting bum rushed by fans. The women were lined up after the games. When we were on the Wyoming-Colorado swing, women actually followed our bus around from Colorado Springs to Denver. It was crazy."

I smiled at the memories.

"That's unbelievable!" Andy said.

It was bananas.

"Yes, it was. After we won the Western Athletic Conference, it took the team literally 2-3 hours to get through the airport."

Andy couldn't believe it. "2-3 hours?"

I laughed.

"Yes. Fans and reporters were everywhere. The city was lit. We had a good season and everybody was getting ready for the NCAA tournament. We were fifth seed in the West. We played in Tucson at the University of Arizona."

"Who did you guys play?" Andy asked.

That game was one I would not soon forget.

"We played George Washington. They had the 7 footer, Inki Dari."

Andy nodded his head. "Right. He was good. How did you guys lose?"

That was a long story.

"Not to make any excuses, but a couple of our guys got food poisoning the night before. We also lost one of our guards to a random drug test. Besides that, they were a good team, and they were better prepared."

Andy whistled. "I wasn't aware of that."

I nodded. Most people weren't.

"It wasn't good luck. I think we would have had a better fight if everybody was healthy. Overall, we had a good season. I had to let bygones be bygones and start getting ready for the NBA."

Andy nodded. "Sure. What NBA teams wanted you most?"

That was easy to answer.

"Boston, Miami, Phoenix, and Indiana. I had no idea the Lakers were looking at me."

Andy was impressed. "Wow!! That's cool."

I smiled.

"Yes, it was. I remember this gentleman from the Lobo Booster Club approached me after our last game against George Washington. He congratulated me and told me that the NBA sent my camp mail to New Mexico State by accident. They'd mistaken me with star guard Sam Crawford.

I was excited when I heard the news. During those times, NBA prospects had to attend two camps and prove themselves before they could be invited to the pre-draft in Chicago. Port Smith, Virginia was one, and the Desert Classic in Phoenix was the other."

Chapter 16: The Betrayal

"How was Port Smith?"

Andy's question was understandable.

"I couldn't tell you. I didn't go."

Now Andy was feeling as confused as I'd felt all those years ago.

"I don't understand."

At the time, I hadn't either.

"I never received my camp mail. Better yet, I wasn't receiving any mail."

Andy looked at me in astonishment.

"I don't understand. You were first team All-WAC, MVP of the WAC, and so on. You mean to tell me you weren't receiving any mail?"

His voice registered the same disgust I'd felt when I figured out what was happening.

"None. At first, I didn't understand. Then, I started putting it all together.

I remember answering the phone one day at the apartment I shared with Khari Jaxon. It was an agent calling for Khari. He asked for my name, and I told him 'Ike Williams." He asked me why I wasn't returning his mail. I'd never received it.

That's when it dawned on me that something wasn't right. I started to question myself. 'Why am I not receiving any mail?'

I knew I'd had a superb season. It didn't make sense that nobody was interested in me. I knew if all failed, I could sign with Larry Johnson's agents. They were recruiting me hard, but in my mind, I knew I had other options. I remember it all like it was yesterday.

I was sitting in the coach's office at New Mexico with Larry Johnson's agents. Since I was optionless and no other agents were interested, at least I thought, I signed. The moment after I signed, my coach at the time pulled stacks and stacks of my mail from his desk, threw it all in the trash, and said, 'I guess we don't need these anymore.'"

Andy looked angry. "Are you serious?"

He wasn't as angry as I felt when I realized what they'd done to me.

"I am. I was devastated. I couldn't believe what I was seeing. Then, I put two and two together. These guys had a deal going on. I forgot that they were coaches at SMU together before SMU got the death penalty in football."

Andy shook his head. "Wow! I can't believe it."

It was still hard for me to believe.

"I couldn't either. Now, though, it made sense why our school manager would sneak me my mail in passing on campus. It would be NBA questionnaires from various NBA teams. They were postdated back months. It didn't look good for me to be sending my questionnaires back late."

Andy interjected. "It could have been mistaken for arrogance."

I nodded.

"Exactly."

Andy was definitely interested in hearing more about this.

"Did you attend the Desert Classic in Phoenix?"

I shook my head.

"I never received my mail."

I could see him trying to figure it out in his head.

"How did you go to the pre-draft in Chicago if you missed those two camps?"

I smiled.

"The NBA sent my invite to Dallas."

Andy whistled. "Wow!! The NBA really wanted to see you. You are not allowed to attend the pre-draft unless you attended Port Smith or the Desert Classic in Phoenix."

It was true.

"Right. I recall talking to an NBA scout at the pre-draft. He asked me why I didn't play in Phoenix. If I would have played in Phoenix, I wouldn't have had to play in Chicago. I would have been drafted from the second round."

Andy's face said it all.

"Really?"

I remember how I felt when the agent told me that.

"Yes. When he told me this, all I could think of was those stacks of letters going into the trash can."

Andy couldn't believe it.

"Wow. Not sending in those questionnaires back on time and missing two camps made you look arrogant."

I nodded my head.

"Exactly."

Andy was scribbling as fast as his fingers could go.

"How did the pre-draft work out?"

That had been a huge blessing.

"Fortunately, it went great. The first three days were physicals and clinics. Ex-NBA players like Reggie Miller from the Indiana Pacers came back and spoke to us about what we would be facing in the NBA."

Andy relaxed a bit and smiled. "That had to be exciting."

It was.

"Everybody who was a potential draft pick was there. If you recall, the 1993 draft was one of the strongest in NBA history."

Andy nodded, remembering the days.

"You're right."

That year, a lot of underclassmen came out.

"Chris Webber, Penny Hardaway, Rodney Rodgers, George Lynch, and many more. With all these underclassmen coming out, those who were on the bubble became free agents."

Andy nodded. "That's tough."

I couldn't help but agree.

"Yes, it was, but I was sure I was going in the top of the second round. Unfortunately, my agents didn't show up at the pre-draft."

Andy stopped me. "Wait a minute. You mean your agents didn't show up?"

I shook my head.

"No, they didn't. I was vulnerable when I interviewed with the Phoenix Suns. I said the wrong thing. When she asked me who the toughest defensive I played against in the WAC was, I answered them honestly. I told them Byron Wilson from Utah. Believe it or not, they drafted him over me."

Andy's eyes got round. "Wow!"

That pretty much summarized the whole situation.

"The night after the draft, I was sick. I'd just bought a teal blue convertible mustang. They didn't call my name. 'What's next?' I asked myself. My mother was crying. She couldn't understand why I was not drafted.

Ironically, Jerry West, General Manager of the Los Angeles Lakers couldn't believe it, either. He called me the next morning and had me on a flight to L.A. Miami didn't want me to go to L.A. They wanted me to be their fifth guard. Mark Aguirre knew Magic Johnson, and he convinced me to go to the Lakers."

"Did you get to see Magic while you were there?" Andy asked.

I grinned.

"Yes. We scrimmaged against Magic and the team he was touring with. He was a sight to see. The things he was doing on the court were unheard of at the time. I remember him coming down court with the ball, spinning, and he went to the hole. He got fouled, but he made it. The crowd went nuts. He came to the bench where I was sitting and whispered in my ear, 'These bit#$@ can't hold me.' It was epic. I couldn't believe he picked me out of all the guys!"

Andy nudged his glasses back up his nose and wrote something down on his notepad. "Incredible."

I could still remember what that felt like.

"He was the highlight of Rookie camp."

Andy had more questions. "How many weeks did Rookie Camp last?"

I held up two fingers.

"Two weeks. The first week we were in Inglewood, California and the second week we were in Irvine, California. The first three days were scrimmages within the team and the next three days we played Portland, Phoenix, Utah, Golden State, and the Clippers."

Andy nodded. "Cool. How did you do?"

I grinned.

"I had a great first week. Jerry West pulled me to the side and told me I was doing good. He was interested in bringing me back for Veteran's Camp. Instantly, I called my agents and informed them of the good news. I told them that I wanted to leave L.A. and go to Miami's rookie camp.

Miami's camps were just starting up, so my agents didn't think it was a good idea. I stayed in L.A. That wasn't a good idea."

Andy paused. "Why?"

I chuckled.

"Politics. The entire second week of camp they iced me. They didn't play me at all, and I couldn't understand why."

Andy looked puzzled.

"Weren't your agents communicating back and forth with the Lakers?"

I shook my head.

"Not to my knowledge."

A look of disgust crept across Andy's face. The room was silent. After a few seconds, I spoke again.

"If I had known better, I would have done away with my agents after the pre-draft. I would have had a better chance. I've learned never, ever to pick an inexperienced agent. My agents were comfortable. Larry Johnson made it easy for them. They didn't have to work hard. An agent proves himself or herself when they can take a player that's on the bubble and get them a shot."

Andy nodded. "You're right. What happened next?"

I shrugged.

"I came back home and continued to work out. I remember being in the club partying and a guy walked up to me and said, 'Congratulations.' I said, 'For what?' He said, 'You didn't know? You were drafted in the third round of the CBA by the Rockford Lightning.'"

Andy shook his head in amazement.

"Your agents didn't tell you?"

I shook my head.

"They didn't."

The room was silent. Then, Andy looked up at me and shook his head again.

"These guys didn't know what they were doing."

I snorted.

"I agree."

Andy's next question was a hard one to answer.

"Were you invited back to veteran's camp?"

The option had been there, but the choice wasn't easy.

"No, I wasn't. I decided to go on to the CBA."

Chapter 17: See It Through

"How was the CBA?" Andy asked.

I was glad he asked.

"It was cool. The CBA had a lot of talent at the time. If you ask me, there was more talent in the CBA than in the NBA."

This seemed to surprise Andy. "Really?"

I nodded my head.

"Yes."

It wasn't hard for me to explain why.

"The guys there were hungry. I recall playing in a CBA tournament in Deer Field, Illinois. One of the players hit the referee for making a bad call. These guys were relentless. They wanted to be called up by the NBA and they would use any means necessary.

It was a good experience for me. I played in Rockford, Illinois. I didn't stay long. The politics were crazy. In the CBA, like so many overseas teams, if you lose 3 or 4 games in a row, they clear the entire roster and start over.

I left the CBA and went overseas to Caracas, Venezuela to play with my college roommate, Khari Jaxon. They needed a guard, and I fit the description. I had one game to prove myself. If I performed well, I stayed. If I didn't, I went back home."

"How did you do?" Andy asked.

I grinned. "I stayed."

Andy and I both laughed at that.

"I think I finished with 38 points that night. Khari and I put on a good show. It was a different experience. They played in outdoor arenas. It put me in mind of the arenas we played in Puerto Rico when I was 12."

Andy nodded. "The culture is different there."

That was an understatement.

"Very. I loved it, though. The people were nice and the women were beautiful. I used to love waking up in the morning and going down to the undergrown market. I couldn't speak Spanish, so I had to buy a book to translate. The only thing I could say was pollo, which meant chicken."

Andy and I broke out laughing again.

"That's all you could say?"

I continued laughing.

"Yes! Unfortunately, chicken was the only thing I was comfortable eating over there. With Venezuela being a 3rd world country, a lot of the food wasn't fresh. In many places, they didn't have running water. It was sad. It made me realize how good we had it in the states. Things we take for granted, they would have died to have. I love the people over there, but I hate how they had to live. When I left Venezuela, I was a different person.

I no longer took things for granted. I went into the USBL focus. I was determined to make the team and get back in the NBA. I played in West Palm Beach, 72.5 miles South of Miami. We played over 36 games in two months. This league was designed to get players ready for NBA camp. Tryouts were ridiculously competitive. There were a hundred players trying out for the team, and they were only keeping 10."

"What?!" Andy looked surprised.

I remembered what it felt like to be in the middle of that.

"Yes, it was tough. Fortunately, tryouts went well. I was told by the coach that I finished number one in the tryouts. I was surprised, because there was some good talent out there. Mark Baker of Ohio state, Rodney Dobard of Florida State, and more. We had a good team, but it started out slow. The first four or five games, I couldn't make a shot, but the coach believed in me.

I remember we were playing in Connecticut and he told me if I stopped shooting, he was going to pull me out. I finally caught my rhythm and from that game on, I averaged 30 plus a game. There was some good talent in the USBL. Anderson Hunt from UNLV was playing for the Miami team and John Lucas was coach at the time.

I watched Hunt play on T.V., but I never played against him. He scored 48 points and I had 36. Everything he shot went in. In the USBL, we had to play the team we were playing three games in a row.

The next two games, he scored 40 plus."

"Wow!!" Andy said.

"This guy was no joke."

I couldn't help but smile as I shook my head at the memories.

"It sounds like you had a great season," Andy said.

I nodded. It had been, too.

"One of the best in my career. To my surprise, nobody picked me up for rookie camp. This was my second time around, and the chances of getting picked were getting slimmer. The new talent was coming out of college, and players were getting moved up from the CBA.

I found it in my best interest to go back to New Mexico and finish my degree. I had one more year left on my scholarship. So, that spring, I moved in with two of my fraternity brothers, Mumbi and Todd. It felt good to be back in New Mexico. Everything went well. I finished the semester off with a 3.0. So I went back home for the Summer. I decided I wasn't going to go back overseas until after I graduated.

Summer was finally over, and I was preparing to go back to New Mexico to finish up school. A week before my plane left, I got a call from the coaches and was told that they couldn't honor my scholarship. I was devastated. I couldn't believe what I was hearing. The scholarship was for five years, not four and a half."

Andy's frustration was evident. "Who were the coaches at New Mexico at the time?"

That was a long time ago, and I saw no point in drudging that back up.

"I'd rather not say. Now, I was forced to get a job. I had no choice. My son was two, soon to be three. I had to do something. Child support was breathing down my back. I started student teaching that semester. I was trying to do everything right to make ends meet. I was back living with my mother, and I was frustrated and lost. The plan was for me to finish school and go back overseas. I couldn't believe what the coaches were doing.

After all I'd done for that school, and they would do this to me? I couldn't understand it. I started to question myself. Why was this happening to me. Was I cursed? For some reason, I couldn't shake the politics. I started to hate basketball. I wanted nothing to do with it anymore.

The pain it brought me was more than I could endure. Basketball was no longer fun. The people who once praised me now despised me. The people who were in my corner suddenly disappeared. The friends that I thought were my friends became my enemies. The women I thought loved me left. I was devastated and went into isolation.

Thank God for Omega Psi Phi Fraternity. It saved my life. It gave me an outlet. The brughs treated me no different. I'm forever indebted to Paul Quinn, the Zeta Eta brughs. They accepted me as if I was one of their own. The brughs treated me no different. They understood what I was going through. The love was unconditional. They were sad when I was sad, and they were happy when I was happy. Me, Box, and Karl spent many days at Paul Quinn. If I was hungry and needed anything, all I had to do was go up to the yard. If the Brughs didn't have it, the Deltas did. It was real brotherhood and sisterhood. That's great."

"You needed that release," Andy said.

It was true. I had needed it.

"I did, but it was time to get back to the real world. I started student teaching, but that was barely paying the bills. I needed more income. I roomed with my brother, Byron. He was paying the majority of the bills, though, and I was starting to become stressed out.

The pressure from my son's mother was starting to become over-whelming. She needed more money for my son. I needed to do some-thing quick, and I did. I panicked. Before I knew it, I finally gave into the very temptations I ran from as a teenager."

Chapter 18: The Dope Game

"I was now in the dope game. I never thought in a million years that I would be selling drugs. I wanted that fast money. Crack wasn't my thing. My spirit wouldn't let me sell it. So, I started to sell marijuana. I remember going to a childhood friend of mine, and telling him I wanted to get in the game. He didn't want to help me, but he knew my situation. So he gave me a pound of marijuana, and a triple beam scale.

He gave me strict orders. He told me to put the scale and the weed in my trunk and go straight home. I was nervous as heck. I couldn't believe I was about to do what I was about to do.

That morning I busted the pound down and bagged it up in dimes. Later, I went out in front of the corner store on Lagow and Hamilton. The rest is history."

Andy stopped me.

"Did you care what people thought of you?"

I could still feel the shame.

"I did. I'll never forget when Monique Mcgee saw me. The look on her face was indescribable. She asked me, 'Boy, what are you doing out here?'"

Andy looked up at me. "What did you say?"

I paused to collect my thoughts.

"I didn't know what to say. I was embarrassed and humiliated. I went from being the neighborhood basketball star to the neighborhood dope boy. I was now a product of the game. The hoop dream was officially over. What people thought didn't matter anymore. My mind was made up. I was going to be in the game."

"Wow! That's amazing how your mind shifted from the court to the streets!!" Andy said.

I had to agree.

"It is mind-blowing how association breeds assimilation. The more you are around something, the more you become it. My mind started to conform, and before I knew it, my image changed. I started to look like a dope boy. I had a black 2-door Eldorado coup on 45 and Vogues, and a Mercedes Benz. Life was good.

I got into real estate with my brother, Byron. He had over 15 or more houses in the neighborhood at the time. He showed me how to flip houses, and before you know it, I had three. I was doing great. At least, I thought was.

I had two women pregnant at the same time. My son's mother was pregnant with my son Isaiah, and my former college girlfriend was pregnant with my daughter, India."

Andy shook his head.

"Whoa!"

I nodded.

"I know. I was spiraling out of control. The women were coming by the dozens. My home life was suffering. I was turning into the one guy I despised."

"Who?" Andy asked.

I grimaced at the memory.

"My father. My relationship at home became abusive. My daughter's mother and I argued and fought just about every night. The police were constantly coming to our house. I regret putting my daughter and her mother through that."

Andy paused for a moment.

"What made you do those things?"

I shrugged. There were no simple answers.

"I was caught up in the lifestyle. I was drinking heavily and getting high off my own supply. I was smoking weed like a freight train. All I wanted was to be in the streets. I was moving up in the ranks in the dope game. I went from selling two to three pounds a week to 50 to a hundred a week. I was now receiving the love I once received when I was playing basketball. Things were going great. Byron and I opened 210 Cuts."

Andy didn't understand.

"What's 210?"

I smiled.

"The last three numbers of our zip code in East Dallas. It was something I thought would be positive for our neighborhood. I named it 210 Cuts. Opening a barbershop, detail, and a studio was my dream at the time.

Byron saw my vision and got behind it. He financed the shop and made sure the business was taken care of while I managed the facility."

Andy gestured toward my tattoo.

"Is that why 210 is on your arm?"

I nodded.

"Sure. Me and a couple of guys in the neighborhood were so excited, we went out the next day and got tattoos. Lil' Felix was first. Then, we did alot of positive things on the corner of Metropolitan and Second. We fed the homeless many days.

210 shined a lot of light on that corner. We shot Quinton Black's Shake Them Haters Off video on the roof of 210."

"Cool," Andy said.

I sighed.

"It was, but home wasn't. Things were getting worse. The arguments and fights were escalating. We were both unhappy. I was spending more time away from the house than I normally did."

Chapter 19: 2 Feet in The Game

"I found myself getting deeper and deeper in the dope game. I was riding around in a different rental car for months. I was dressing in the best clothes. I had women all over town. I was living the life.

Before I left the barbershop every night, I would stop on Baldwin to see my chick. She was about six feet, slim, and chocolate. We sat outside every night and we would smoke a blunt before I went home. She knew how to take my mind off of things. Some nights, she used to take me to places I'd never been. It was a level of ecstasy I'd never felt.

She was my ride or die. She gave me an offer I couldn't refuse. She invited me to go to a place I'd never been. I took the offer. We were now turned out to the game. We were now in the lifestyle where pimps played and hoes hoed. This game chose me, I didn't choose it. As I played the game, though, I realized that the game I was playing was no longer for me."

Andy looked confused. I could understand.

"You were a pimp?"

I shrugged and tried to explain.

"I tried my hand at it. It was something she wanted. She asked me to do. I didn't refuse. I was always curious about it, but it wasn't for me. It called for time I didn't have. I became so consumed with the game, I forgot about home. My home was being neglected, and some-one else was paying attention."

Andy interrupted.

'What was the straw that broke the camel's back at home?"

I shook my head.

"I fell asleep one night without locking my phone. She went into my messages and heard my friend on Baldwin say that the condom broke and she was pregnant. My daughter's mother left a couple of weeks after that. It was the best thing for us, because I was spiraling out of control in the dope gang.

I was becoming a target. Our house was no longer safe for a family.

I was keeping large amounts of money and the drugs in the house at times. It was best that we went our separate ways. It wasn't fair to try to stop her from leaving. She deserved to be happy. We were both unfaithful to each other.

The hardest thing for me at the time was that I wasn't going to wake up to my daughter in the morning. No more watching the Lion King when I came in late nights."

Andy was sympathetic.

"That had to be tough."

Tough didn't begin to describe it.

"It was. The thought of my four-year-old daughter being around another man was devastating. When they left, I became numb. I started to slip in the game. I started to make mistakes. Word on the street was that I was on the radar of the authorities.

The sources were valid. Friends of the family that was on the police force sent word to my family. They say I sold dope to an undercover officer. I was to be busted at any time. I found that not to be true. I knew that if they really had something on me, they would have made their move.

Older hustlers taught me to always keep you circle tight, and never go outside you circle for anything. I did just that.

I later found out through another source that the police had pictures of my car. The first mistake I made was when I drove my Mercedes-Benz to East Dallas for the Hamilton Avenue block party. From that day on, I never drove my Mercedes-Benz to East Dallas any more. I bought an old Delta 88, with no hub caps or air conditioning. The hood was a different color from the rest of the car. I had to wise up and go under the radar.

I only drove my Mercedes-Benz at night or on the weekends. Either I was going to GG's, Iguana Mirage, The Filling Station, or Rich and Big Glen's house. Rich and Glen were my fraternity brothers. They lived in Hamilton Park. Their house was like a casino. Every night it was a party. Either they were shooting dice or betting on the games. The women were around for entertainment. The rules of the house, any things goes.

We switched houses every weekend. Either we were at Rich and Glen's, or we were at my house in Mesquite. The party never stopped. One weekend at my house, we lit the Barbeque grill on Friday and it went out on Sunday."

Andy laughed.

"Are you kidding me?"

I shook my head.

"No. We called it the 91 weekend. Nobody went home."

Andy couldn't believe it.

"What did your neighbors say?"

I laughed.

"Nothing. They partied with us."

Andy shook his head in amazement.

"Wow!! You guys were rock stars."

It sure felt that way.

"Pretty much. It took my mind off the streets momentarily, but the pain and numbness I was feeling still existed. I was stressed. The authorities were still breathing down my neck. I had to think of a master plan.

I enrolled in an A+ certification computer class down by the projects. My friend, Omar, had a nonprofit, and he let me enroll. This was
a tactic I used to get the authorities off my scent."

Andy looked up.

"Did it work?"

I shook my head.

"Not really. Every now and then, I would see police show up at my
class. Eventually, they would leave and at lunch I would make my
rounds. I would come back to class as if nothing happened. In no way
am I condoning selling drugs. I didn't get in the game for the fortune
and fame. I got in the game to feed my family. I always understood
that the streets were a dead end. There's only two ways out: death or
jail. And I was heading for both."

Andy twirled his pen.

"Wow!"

That didn't begin to summarize it.

"The streets are real and dangerous. I remember one day, my cousin Nikel and I were at a stop light in my Mercedes-Benz on MLK and Meadow in South Dallas. We had the music up and the windows down. A Delta 88 pulled up next to us at the light. The driver got out of the car headed towards the hood. My instincts kicked in and I pressed on the gas and ran through the light. I forgot that my Glock .9mm was under my hood."

Andy leaned forward.

"What happened next?"

I could still remember that cold chill that ran down my spine.

"I looked back through the rear-view mirror and saw him running back to his car with an uzi machine gun in his hand. I took a right on Robert B. Cullum and ran through the light on Pennsylvania. He was on my tail like a cat on a rat.

The 18 inch rims that were on my Mercedes were preventing me from moving any faster. I gambled. I acted as if I were going right, but took a sharp left up the one way on Fitzhugh. He kept going, and I escaped."

Andy breathed a sigh of relief.

"You were lucky."

I nodded.

"I was. Unfortunately, I didn't learn my lesson."

Andy leaned back to listen.

"Why do you say that?"

I took a deep breath.

"One night, my childhood friend, KK, and I were leaving Cry Babies. Cry Babies was a strip club in South Dallas. It was run mafia style. The girls were dancing in the front and the hustlers were shooting dice on the pool tables in the back."

"Whoa," Andy said. "What happened next?"

I continued my story.

"Once I dropped KK off at home on Beaman Street, I stopped at a gas station on the hill in East Dallas. Normally, I don't stop late at night at gas stations, but on that night I did. I was slipping, and it almost cost me my life."

"How?" Andy asked.

I thought about how lucky I'd been that night.

"I was sitting in my car, looking through my CD case, getting ready to pull out of the gas station. Something told me to look up and look out the rear-view mirror. I did just that. I saw two guys getting out of an old '64 Impala walking up on my car. They both had sawed-off shotguns in their hands. If I would have looked up a minute later, I would have been robbed or killed."

Andy shook his head.

"Unbelievable."

Life changing was a better word for it.

"After these two incidents, I started to look at things differently. I knew if I didn't slow down, I was going to end up dead or in jail. I was ready to give it all up and find something new to do. I did just that. I walked away from it all.

I got rid of my house, my Mercedes-Benz, and anything else I acquired while I was in the dope game."

Chapter 20: Game Over

"I left the game, never to return. I got into the music business with my fraternity brother, Mo B. Dick."

Andy laughed.

"His name was Mo B. Dick?"

I smiled.

"Yes. He was one of the music producers for No Limit Records. He was part of a production team called Beats By the Pound."

Andy nodded.

"Oh, ok."

I went on.

"In the late 90's and early 2000's, No Limit Records was the biggest rap label in the world. During their reign, Mo B. and I always stayed in contact. He always told me if things didn't work out with Master P., we would put our minds together and see what we could come up with. Unfortunately, things didn't work out for him at No Limit, so he left."

Andy looked up from his notepad.

"How did you guys reconnect?"

I smiled.

"One night, I was at Que Daug's party in North Dallas. Mo B., Cane & Abel, and Cat Daddy from K104 showed up looking for me. Shortly after that, we were at the drawing table putting a project together.

At that time, I had no access to a studio, but my childhood friend, Hard, did. His studio was in a duplex on Collins Street in East Dallas. One side he lived in and the other side was his studio. We recorded the majority of the album with his group, G Related."

Andy stopped his pen for a second.

"What was the name of your group?"

I laughed.

"210. The compilation was named T.B.K.S for Texas's Best Kept Secret. Mo B. put the project together and did the production. My job was to handle the business."

Andy nodded.

"Cool."

I went on.

"Getting into the music business was something I'd always wanted to do. I was excited about the project. This was my second chance, my way out. I put everything I had into this project. I made many sacrifices. Some paid off. Some didn't. I have no regrets, but one."

Andy looked up.

"What was that?"

I sighed and shook my head.

"The time I spent away from my kids. I missed a lot of their teenage years chasing the dream. I wanted them to have a brighter future. I didn't want them to experience the things I experienced as a child. I didn't want them to grow up in poverty, so I put it all on the line. It was all or nothing.

I was grinding harder than ever before in my life. There were many sleepless nights. At any given time, Mo B. and I were either in Dallas, Baton Rouge, or Wichita, Kansas. We were working the project nonstop. Dallas and Baton Rouge was where the business was handled. Wichita, Kansas was where we went to regroup."

Andy looked puzzled.

"Why Wichita?"

That was a good question.

"We would go to Wichita and visit our fraternity brothers. The E Psi brughs took care of us. Chubs, Wee, Karl, Box, JJ, Wayne, Jamie, Leo, Big Troy, and so many more made it easy for us to cross that bridge.

We had some great times in Wichita. The mutt session was unbelievable. The people were great, but we had to go. We had to get back to business, back to the drawing board. We had a project to promote, and the money was running out.

Mo B. was going through legal issues with Master P., and I had no income coming in. I was out of the dope game, and I refused to go back, so I moved back home with my mother."

"What was it like having to go back to your mom's house?" Andy asked.

I shook my head.

"It was difficult. I was used to being on my own. I was accustomed to the suburban lifestyle. Now, I was back in the hood. I had to get readjusted. I had to deal with the hate and ridicule from people who had started to lose respect for me. They didn't understand that I went home by choice, not because I couldn't make it. I did it all for the cause. Unfortunately, people didn't get it, but we stayed focused and kept it moving.

On the other hand, we had a large number of supporters. The community was behind us all the way. They wanted to see us make it. They supported everything we did. The T.B.K.S. basketball league was standing room only. Over one hundred people followed us out of town for our promo shows. Our buzz was growing, as well as the hate. People who didn't believe in the movement at its beginning stages wanted in now.

A lot of tension started forming in the community. The neighborhood was in turmoil. My little cousin, Stacy, found out some devastating news about his mother and killed the ice cream man. Word on the street was that it was self-defense. Unfortunately, the D.A. didn't see it that way. They gave him a life sentence. He was only 16 years old."

Andy shook his head in disbelief.

"Wow!"

I went on with the story.

"Things were starting to take a turn for the worse. People in my family were starting to die. We lost my cousin, Sonya, my uncle, Lee Roy, my grandmother, Susie, and my Aunt Jean."

Andy shook his head again as he listened.

"Wow!! How did you maintain your sanity?"

It was difficult.

"If it wasn't for my girlfriend, Nicole, I probably would have lost it. I never met a woman like her before. I never met a woman that stood behind her man like she did. The way she supported me was indescribable.

We met one night in the parking lot across from GG's Night club on Northwest Highway. Mo B and I were coming back from Kansas in Big Kevin's Expedition. I saw this beautiful, light skinned Canadian woman, with a butt like Serena Williams walking through the parking lot. I called her to the car. We exchanged numbers, and we were together for the next 5 years.

She was a blessing in disguise. Words can't describe the deeds of this woman. She was virtuous. She moved me out my mother's house into the White Rock Resorts and later to a town home in Addison. She even bought me a car. I regret that I didn't marry her."

"Why didn't you?" Andy asked.

It was hard to explain.

"I didn't want to be selfish. Her dream was to run her own boarding school, and her dream came true. She was offered a Director's position at a boarding school in Maryland. I didn't want to get in the way of that."

"Why didn't you go with her?" Andy asked.

That had been a painful decision.

"I wanted to, but I couldn't leave my kids. They were still young."

Andy nodded.

"I see. That had to be tough for you."

Tough didn't begin to describe it.

"It was. We stayed the night with each other. She met me for breakfast before she left. That day was one of the saddest days of my life."

"Did you guys keep in touch with each other after she left?" Andy asked.

I sighed.

"We did for a while. We decided it would be better if we let go and go our separate ways."

Andy nodded, and the look on his face said it all.

"I'm sorry to hear that."

I was silent for a moment before continuing.

"Thanks. I still think about her to this day. She wasn't just my lover. She was my friend. She understood me in a way nobody else did. She saved me from self-destructing in my neighborhood at the time."

Andy seemed to understand. "She was really special."

I nodded.

"She was. She was there for me when nobody else was. If it wasn't for her, and the road trips Mo. B and I took to Kansas and Baton Rouge, I probably would have lost my mind."

Chapter 21: Knowledge of Self

"How was Baton Rouge?" Andy asked.

I thought about the best way to answer that question.

"Baton Rouge was nice. I had a hard time getting adjusted to the culture."

Andy looked interested.

"Why?"

It wasn't easy to say why.

"Southern Louisiana has its own identity. It's like New York in a sense. They do things their own way. Their culture was like no other. Everything was different. The food, the lingo, and the vibration was one-of-a-kind. The people and even their very consciousness of what was going on in the world was all unique.

It was the first time I saw guys that came from the hood reading on a constant basis. I can remember being on the south side of Baton Rouge with my fraternity brother, Aron. They called it the bottom, and it was a neighborhood similar to the neighborhood I grew up in as a kid. We were at Aron's house.

Mo B. and I spent a lot of time over there when we were away from the studio. The conversations there were great. We would sit on the porch and talk with the older guys in the community about awareness and change, and what was going on in the world.

We would watch great historians speak on our history and where we came from. It was beautiful to see guys that looked like me and came from where I came from read. It was great. I had a spiritual awakening.

When I left Louisiana and came back to Texas, I had a knowledge of self."

Andy stopped his pen.

"That's great that you were exposed to guys that read. That's rare."

I couldn't have agreed more.

"That's true. I remember watching Craig B reading Malachi York books around the studio at KLC's house."

Andy stopped me.

"Who are Craig B and KLC?"

I laughed.

"They are also members of Beats By the Pound. I was inspired by seeing those guys read. I used to watch how Fiend and Odell studied the music business, and I realized from that point on that if I was going to be a good business man, I had to read.

Many of the books I read today, I first saw lying around Fiend's office in his studio, Crack Alley."

Andy looked up from his notepad.

"What's Crack Alley?"

I realized how strange that must have sounded to Andy and chuckled.

"That was the name of his studio."

Andy nodded.

"Oh, okay. Who is Fiend and Odell?"

I smiled.

"Fiend was a recording artist for No Limit Records at the time. Odell was the fourth member of Beats By The Pound. Odell pretty much handled the business for Beats By The Pound. I used to love to watch him work. He used to let me sit in on some of his conference calls with Wendy Day.

She was helping them sell their beats at the time. Wendy helped Cash Money with their first big deal with Universal. She was the lady of the music industry at the time."

"Wow!!" Andy said.

I had to agree.

"Yes. I was fortunate to be able to see business handled at that level. It was unbelievable. I remember going to sleep and waking up watching these guys work in the studio. It was genius. I never saw anything like it in my life. The way those guys worked together was inexplicable. The beats and the production were incredible.

The knowledge, wisdom, and understanding I was getting from being around these guys I did not take for granted. I knew it was something special. I knew I was around greatness. I learned a lot of things just from being around them.

Odell asked me to ride to the store with them. He told me some things that changed my viewpoint in life."

"What did he say?" Andy asked.

I could still remember that day. It was a turning point for me.

"He told me I was special, and that I had a gift I didn't recognize at the time. He told me that the things that came natural to me in the music business were difficult for the average person to do.

He explained to me how he worked with Master P and Baby and Slim of Cash Money Records. He felt like I had similar qualities to those guys. He helped me to understand how hard it was for people to create a buzz and get a music project hot. His words help me identify with who I was and what I could become in the music business. So yes, being around these guys, I learned how the music business really went.

I would sit back and watch how seriously KLC took his craft. This guy never smiled. He was game face at all times."

"Who was KLC?" Andy asked.

"He was the fourth member of Beats By The Pound. Being around these guys was a great experience for me. They showed me a lot of love. Tough love, at times, but I never complained. I had to learn the protocol for how things were supposed to go. It was difficult at times, because I was getting a crash course in the music business. Things were moving fast, and I had to keep up.

Guys like Mr. Serv On would sit me down at KLC's house and brief me on the music business. He would tell me the things he'd learned from Master P. about how to make it in the music business."

"Wow!! That was cool of him," Andy said.

I couldn't agree more, and I could never thank that man enough.

"It was. Mr. Serv On is like a big brother to me. He always showed me love. I remember we all went to the All-Star game in Atlanta. He made sure I didn't want for anything. He showed me how the music industry really went, if you know what I mean.

I remember sitting down and having a conversation with him at a restaurant. He asked me, 'Why are you not excited by what's going on around you?' He didn't realize at the time that I had played college and professional ball, and I was familiar with the environment. From that point, it made all the sense in the world to him. He smiled at me and said, "I used to watch you play late night at New Mexico."

"That's cool," Andy said.

It was.

"How was the experience in Atlanta?" Andy asked.

It was different. Normally, when I went to super bowls or All-Star games, I went for the parties and the women. It wasn't like that with these guys. It was strictly business. We were on the move constantly. We were either in the studio with David Banner and the Nappy Roots, or handling business at BMI.

It was all business. When we ate lunch with Killer Mike and Devin, it was all business. The highlight of the trip was when we signed a promotion and distribution deal with Southwest Records. It felt good to be in that room, sitting around the table, watching the good responses while the executives listen to our project, T.B.K.S. This was a great trip.

When I left Atlanta, I had a better understanding of what the music business was like. All business and no play."

I looked at Andy.

"I see," Andy said. "Sounds like the exposure was great there for you."

"It was," I replied. "Almost greater than meeting J. Prince of Rap Alot Records."

"Oh, really? Tell me more," Andy said.

So I did.

"I went to Houston one weekend with Beats By The Pound on business. They were meeting up with J. Prince. This was the first time I met David Banner. He was there also. He was selling his beats at the time. He was on his hustle.

This was before the music deal. He was riding around in a Camero at the time. I was inspired by his hustle. I saw him before the millions. After he got his big deal, I knew at that point that dreams do come true."

"That's true," Andy said. "What was it like being around J.Prince for the first time?"

I smiled at the memories that question brought up for me.

"It was a sight to see. We met up with him at his mother's house in the 5th Ward of Houston. He pulled up in a yellow Lamborghini. He took us to a two-story servant's quarters behind his mother's house where we sat around and talked for a while.

Then, Shockley asked me what my name was and where I was from, so I told him. Everything was cool. We left there and followed him to their music studio, The Compound. As we were leaving his mom's house, he made a couple of stops in the neighborhood. He got out of his Lamborghini like it was nothing, went to the door, and had a conversation with an elderly woman as if he'd never left the neighborhood. At that point, my level of respect for J. Prince escalated.

That was real to me. This man was one of the biggest moguls in the music industry, and was still humble. He didn't let the fame or the money consume him. He never forgot where he came from and the people of Houston loved him for that.

That was the highlight of my trip, besides sitting in The Compound while he listened to our project, T.B.K.S. To start a project from scratch and see it manifest into the hands of J. Prince was incredible."

Chapter 22: The Disappointment

"I was on a high when we got back to Baton Rouge, until Mo B. and I were pulled over by the police. That was a scary situation.

We had marijuana in the car, and the police found it. They let me go, but unfortunately Mo B. had some business with the courts he had to clear up.

He was gone for some months, so I had to pack up and go back to Dallas. When I got back home, things were chaotic.

The group was falling apart. Some of the guys went to jail. The other guys joined another rap label.

I tried everything I could to keep the movement going. I even got into film.

Every day in the neighborhood, I had my camera. I was putting a documentary together. Film was now my newfound passion. I was filming and editing everything I touched.

I started off with the Hamilton Avenue Block Parties DVDS. I didn't know what I was doing at the time, but everybody, for the most part, liked what I was doing.

However, I knew in my mind that I needed to get some revenue coming in. So, I had to put the camera down.

Now, I was back to square one. I was devastated. All that I sacrificed and gave up was all in vain. Five years away from my kids and my loved ones flushed down the drain.

My house I once had was gone. I had to start back over with nothing. I had to do one of the most humiliating things I ever did in my life."

"What was that?" Andy asked.

I could still feel the pain of that moment.

"I had to knock on my mother's door and tell her I needed a place to stay. I had nothing but an old Honda Accord my ex-girlfriend, Nicole, bought me. I had no idea I would end up on my mother's couch after all the blood, sweat, and tears I put into the music.

It was tough. There was nothing easy about going back to my mother's house. The tension between the two of us was getting thick. At the time, I had no income coming in. I had to come up with a plan to get out of my mother's house, and quick. I was 38 years of age at the time. Sleeping on my mother's couch was no place for a grown man.

The frustration started to increase. Things weren't happening as quickly as I wanted them to. The pressure and depression were taking their toll. I didn't know what to do at the time. I refused to go back to the street life. I'd made a promise to myself that I would never sell drugs again, but believe me, the temptation was there."

Andy nodded.

"I'm sure it was."

I nodded and went on with the story.

"I wasn't accustomed to being broke, so I tried selling cars. My childhood friend, Keno, was the lead salesman at Trophy Nissan at the time. He introduced me to the car business. He influenced the managers and encouraged them to give me a shot. They did.

I had a hard time getting adjusted. The depression was taking its toll, and my energy levels were low. I wasn't happy. I wasn't in a great place in life, and my numbers showed it.

My focus was more on the night life, as opposed to my job. I was partying, drinking, and smoking weed more than ever. I was spending more time in the strip clubs, where I was picking up more bad habits. My fraternity brother and I would go to Dallas Gentleman's at least four or five nights out of the week. He was a lawyer, so we had the money to party like rock stars.

There were times we would go to the club and his tab would be five thousand dollars. The strippers would argue over who was going to go home with us for the night. We would leave the club and go back to my frat brother's house and have wild parties. We would smoke marijuana, drink, take ecstasy, and have wild sex."

Andy stopped writing and looked up, shaking his head.

"Wow!! That was a lot. What made you go to the extreme?"

I was not proud of those moments.

"This was my escape from depression and the stress that I was under. It took my mind off of the pain."

Andy nodded.

"How long did you party like that?"

I shrugged.

"About two years in a row. I finally got burnt out. The fast lane was taking its toll on me. My production at work was inconsistent. One week, I would sell a lot of cars. The next week, I would bomb.

I was going nowhere fast. My mentors, Rabbit, Money Mike, and Hollywood, told me I needed to slow down and come up with a plan.

Rabbit's favorite words were, 'Don't be in a hurry to make a mistake.'"

Andy adjusted his glasses.

"Profound."

I had to agree. It was.

Chapter 23: The Ten Year Plan

"I decided to take their advice. I decided to make some changes and get my life together. I reverted back to what I learned back in Louisiana. I started reading and studying every day. I started to eat right. I was on a strict regimen. No more pork, no more beef. Just chicken and fish. I started juicing and meditating every day.

Before I knew it, I was back on my spiritual path. The desire for marijuana and black and milds went away."

"That's great!" Andy said. "You really started to turn your life around."

I nodded my agreement.

"I was destined for change. I was focused once again. I realized the car business wasn't for me. I decided to enroll in truck driving school.

I needed something that would complement the style of living that I was accustomed to.

I was accustomed to fast money, and the car business wasn't fast enough for me. I came up with a ten-year plan. I started reading books by Jim Rohn, Zig Ziglar, and many other motivational speakers on goal setting and ways to build a successful business. Educating myself was the best thing I ever did for myself. It changed my way of thinking and put me on a path to success."

"I agree," Andy said. "You made a 360 degree turn."

I had to agree.

"I did. My level of consciousness went from zero to one hundred. I credit it all to reading, meditation, prayer, and proper diet."

"What were some of the books you were reading?" Andy asked.

"I read a variety of books. I started off reading self-help books like Think And Grow Rich, As A Man Thinketh, Rich Dad, Poor Dad, The Alchemists, and The Celestine Prophecy. Those were some of my favorites."

Andy was nodding his head as I listed the titles.

"Wow!! Those are great books."

I smiled.

"They are. They changed my life. Reading really is fundamental."

Andy nodded. "Do you still read a lot?"

I shook my head.

"Not as much as I used to. The first two years I was driving over the road, I would read maybe two or three books a week. I would listen to the audio versions of the books, and it made time go by fast while I was driving."

"Cool!!" Andy said. "How was the trucking industry?"

My smile deepened.

"I loved it. It was the best thing to happen to me at the time. I needed to get away from everything. Being over the road gave me time to reflect on a lot of things in my life. I put a lot of things in perspective while I was out there."

"It was a form of healing for you," Andy said.

It truly was.

"I agree. I made that truck work to my advantage. I made it my office, my sanctuary, and my home. I didn't listen to the radio. I used that time to study business. My phone was my T.V., and YouTube was my best friend. I learned marketing and how to structure my own businesses. I studied every entrepreneur from Rap Moguls to Fortunate 500 executives.

I did this over a five-year period. I had a 10 year plan. The first five years was to position myself as well as educate myself in business. My first goal was to get a better car. I needed reliable transportation. My second goal was to get off my mother's couch and get my own place. Once I accomplished these two things, the other goals I set weren't that difficult."

"What were the other goals?" Andy asked.

That was a great question.

"My third goal was to revitalize my credit. My fourth goal was to write my book and start my businesses."

"What businesses?" Andy asked.

I was so glad he asked.

"First, I started my own publishing company, U Can LLC. Second, I started my non-profit, Unlocked Mindz, Inc. Third, I started my t-shirt line. Fourth, I started Nafsi Logisitics LLC. Nafsi Logistics is a brokering and trucking company."

Andy stopped me. "Tell me more about your businesses."

"U Can publishing will be a host for unpublished authors to tell their story."

"Any movies are documentaries," Andy said with a smile.

I chuckled.

"I don't want to speak too early on that. My lawyers would kill me."

Andy grinned.

"Come on, you can tell me."

I shook my head, but I smiled at him.

"I'm going to say it like this. Don't be surprised if you do."

Andy let it go. "Enough said. Tell me more about Unlocked Mindz."

This was a pet project of mine.

"Unlocked Mindz is the non-profit. It was created for awareness and change, wellness and health. We put together two programs that I felt would help prevent kids from making the mistakes I made. The first program is called Plan B. Plan B is a two-day clinic that would run throughout the summer. We will have a variety of speakers coming in and educating the athletes on awareness and change plus health and wellness.

We will also be assisting athletes in the recruiting process. It's important that they are educated. We want to make sure they make the best decisions while choosing the college they want to attend."

"Cool," Andy said.

I continued.

"The next program is called You Can Do It. You Can Do It is an SAT/ ACT program. This is vital for athletes, especially for those in the inner city. If athletes are better equipped for these tests, it will prevent them from making the terrible mistakes I made in life."

"That's wonderful!" Andy said.

I smiled. It felt good to know I could take my experiences and use them to help others.

"Thanks. Nafsi Logistics speaks for itself. It's a brokering and trucking company."

"What inspired you to open a trucking company?" Andy asked.

That was a very good question.

"An older friend of mine, Rodney. I watched him take one truck and turn it into a fleet of ten and more. He now grosses over $2 million dollars a year. When I came off the road, I joined his company. This was a great opportunity for me to learn the business from the ground up, and I did just that.

I watched him closely and I learned from the things he did right as well as from the things he did wrong. I was fortunate to have the on-the-job training. Seeing him do what he did with his company inspired me to want to have my own. Now, I have Nafsi Logistics. It's still under construction, and will be launched in the near future."

"Cool," Andy said. "I'm proud of you, Isaac. You made your past work for you. This was a great interview, and I appreciate you inviting me to your house. By the way, I love your high rise. The view is great."

I appreciated his words, but I didn't want to take credit I didn't deserve.

"Thank you. God is good. If it wasn't for God, none of this would be possible. Second chances are rare in the world, and I appreciate God's grace for giving me another one."

Andy nodded.

"That's true. Maybe we can come back and do a second interview on the second half of your ten-year plan."

I smiled. That was a great idea!

"I would love that. Maybe we could name it, The After Math: From the Courts To The Streetz."

"That would be great," Andy said. "Oh, by the way, you forgot to tell us about your book."

I laughed.

"You're reading it."

Andy chuckled and shook my hand.

"Thanks a lot. It's been a pleasure."

I was grateful for Andy's help in getting this work finished.

"Thank you."

About the Author

Isaac "Ike-Moe" Williams was born and raised in Dallas, Texas, the youngest child of 5 siblings. He grew up in the projects and made an early name for himself playing basketball.

After being recruited to the University of New Mexico and playing for 3 years on the Lobos basketball team, he eventually made his way to the Los Angeles' Lakers.

When his career with the Lakers ended, he spent time playing in overseas leagues before coming back home to Dallas. His struggles to make ends meet led him into the street life. It nearly killed him, but he managed to make it out.

Today, he is the owner of several businesses, including a non-profit called Unlocked Mindz which is designed to help athletes avoid the same issues and struggles he went through when he was younger.

Connect with him online:

Unlocked Mindz: https://www.facebook.com/Unlockedmindz/

51785743R00105

Made in the USA
San Bernardino, CA
01 August 2017